JAPANESE FAN PAINTINGS
from Western Collections

JAPANESE FAN PAINTINGS
from Western Collections

Selection and Introductory Essay by Kurt A. Gitter
Notes to the Plates by Pat Fister

New Orleans Museum of Art • 1985

Cover: No. 8, Nakamura Hōchū, *Screen of Fan Paintings* (detail).

The exhibition and catalog for *Japanese Fan Paintings from Western Collections* were made possible by grants from The Commemorative Association for the Japan World Exposition (1970) and the Japan-United States Friendship Commission.

Exhibition schedule:

New Orleans Museum of Art   June 15-September 8, 1985
Asian Art Museum of San Francisco   October 8, 1985-January 5, 1986

Library of Congress Cataloging in Publication Data

Gitter, Kurt A., 1937-
    Japanese fan paintings from western collections.

    Bibliography: p.
    1. Fan painting, Japanese—Edo period, 1600-1868—Exhibitions. 2. Fan painting—Collectors and collecting—United States—Exhibitions. 3. Fan painting—Collectors and collecting—European—Exhibitions. I. Fister, Pat, 1953-   . II. Title.
ND1053.5.G57 1985   759.952′074′016335   84-19097
ISBN 0-89494-021-X

FOREWORD AND ACKNOWLEDGEMENTS

As an ardent collector of Japanese art for more than twenty years, I have always been intrigued by the intimate and personal character of Japanese fan paintings. These small-scaled works of art often represented pinnacles of expression by many of the major and minor artists of the Edo period.

Realizing the beauty and uniqueness of this art form, I began to acquire fan paintings early in my collecting career and have continued to do so. Several years ago, it occurred to me that no English language monograph or exhibition catalog had been solely devoted to Japanese fan paintings of the Edo period. Aware that many fine fans had been on the art market in Japan since 1945, I assumed that excellent examples could now be found both in public and private collections in the West.

With that premise, I wrote to all of the major Western museums and collectors, describing my intent to publish a book on Japanese fans from Western collections and to have these objects presented in an exhibition organized by the New Orleans Museum of Art.

The response from museums and collectors was dramatic. More than 350 fan paintings were evaluated either in person or by photograph. Of these, over fifty were finally selected to represent the best examples of Edo period fan paintings outside of Japan. I decided to include only individual works by known artists of the Edo period, and to limit the selection to fans from the Rimpa, Nanga, and Shijō schools. The intent of this publication is to present the distinctive beauty of this art form, and to allow broader public exposure and enjoyment of these objects.

I reviewed all of the available Western references on Japanese fan paintings and, with the aid of Joseph Seubert of Tokyo, translated into English the most important treatises on this subject published in Japanese. With this information, the introductory essay and historical perspective on fan paintings were formulated for this publication.

Dr. Pat Fister, formerly Research Fellow of Japanese Art at the New Orleans Museum of Art and currently Curator of Oriental Art at the Spencer Museum, University of Kansas, has written the commentaries, with translations of the inscriptions, on each of the works selected to insure a high level of academic accuracy. She also assisted with the overall organization of the exhibition. Dr. Fister is pleased to acknowledge the assistance of Sasaki Jōhei, Yabumoto Sōshirō, Deguchi Midori, and Joseph Tsenti Chang in reading difficult inscriptions and seals. Dr. Stephen Addiss, Roger Green, and Alice Rae Yelen also aided me in editing the introductory essay.

E. John Bullard, Director of the New Orleans Museum of Art, encouraged this project from the start and supported its development. I am grateful to both the New Orleans Museum of Art and the Asian Art Museum of San Francisco, under the able direction of René-Yvon Lefebvre d'Argencé, for agreeing to present *Japanese Fan Paintings from Western Collections*. On their behalf, I am pleased to thank the many museums and private collectors who have generously lent to the exhibition and who have permitted their fans to be reproduced in this publication.

I am delighted to acknowledge the support received from The Commemorative Association for the Japan World Exposition (1970) and the Japan-United States Friendship Commission. The grants from these two organizations supported both the exhibition and the publication.

Although the selection of fans reflects the opinions of many noted scholars in the United States and Japan, I assume all responsibility for the final choice of art works included in this publication; also for the material and opinions expressed in the introductory essay, and any inherent controversies contained therein.

KURT A. GITTER, M.D.

JAPANESE FANS: AN INTRODUCTION

The study of Japanese fan paintings provides a glimpse into the creative experiences of Japanese artists through the centuries since fan paintings reflect the prevalent artistic currents of the times in which they were created. Although the themes and painting techniques of fans are often similar and related to concurrent scroll and screen paintings, the unique format and shape of the fan provide alternative solutions for individual creativity through compositional design.

This publication contains many of the best examples of Japanese fan paintings in Western collections by artists of three of the most important schools of painting that flourished during the Edo period: Rimpa, Nanga, and Shijō. The majority of these fans were acquired by their present owners in Japan during the past thirty years, when fine art was abundant and selective buying was possible. I did not include any of the numerous anonymous fans from the Kanō and Tosa schools, since these works were primarily mass produced in workshops for utilitarian purposes within Japanese society. Likewise Ukiyo-e and Zen fan paintings were excluded since only a handful of fine examples of the former and none of the latter were found in Western collections.

Fan paintings are artworks in which painters use the distinctive shape of the fan to create individual expressions in ink or color. There are basically two kinds of fans in Japan: one is the round, the other wedge or crescent shaped. The round shaped fan *(uchiwa)* was recorded earlier and is Chinese in origin. The wedge-shaped fan *(hiogi)* was originally made of folding wooden blades of Japanese cypress, which were fastened at one end and tied loosely with strings at the other, so as to spread open in a radiating arch. The folding fan is generally considered to be indigenous to Japan even though controversy over its true origin still exists. Nevertheless, the folding fan was exported from Japan to China beginning in the Nara period (A.D. 645-794), gaining great popularity on the mainland during the Song Dynasty (A.D. 960-1279).

In Japan, fans were probably originally purely utilitarian, used for cooling in the summer; later they were used also for ceremonial functions. The first fans were made of wood and not painted. Later, fans were made of paper and enhanced with calligraphy and/or painting. The term *ogie* describes fan painting.

The union of function with beauty, a hallmark of Japanese aesthetics, is particularly noteworthy in the production of fans. Since fans were functional as practical items, they became consumable objects and were either worn out or destroyed in time. Thus, relatively few survived, especially from the 7-13th centuries. By the end of the Muromachi (1334-1573) and Momoyama (1573-1615) periods and certainly throughout the Edo period (1615-1868), many of the fan paintings created by the leading individual artists fortunately were preserved. This undoubtedly reflected public and private admiration for these objects, which were collected and cherished for hundreds of years.

As fan paintings are relatively small, they display an intimacy between the artist and viewer that is often lacking in larger hanging scrolls or screens. Fans are best appreciated (in their utilitarian stage) when held in the viewer's hand and examined three dimensionally, with a slight rotation of the fan handle. One can frequently sense the personal creative energy of the artist in these fans, just as one can appreciate Rembrandt's great genius in his drawings more immediately than in his paintings. Although the fan is invariably associated with the Orient, it inspired many 19th century European artists, including Gauguin and Degas, to create fan designs of their own.

Fan painting formats differ from the horizontal picture planes of handscrolls and the vertical shapes of hanging scrolls, requiring creative design solutions. The most important consideration is a compositional problem: how can a skillful painting be made to respond to the unique shape of the fan? The important elements unique to the horizontal fan format are its curved and arched upper and lower borders, plus the fan's radiance. The latter term is used to explain the fan structure, whereby radiating lines, formed by the wooden ribs, originate from a focal point below the fan surface, and divide the fan into numerous, narrow sections. The final consideration in the horizontal fan is the visual impact the

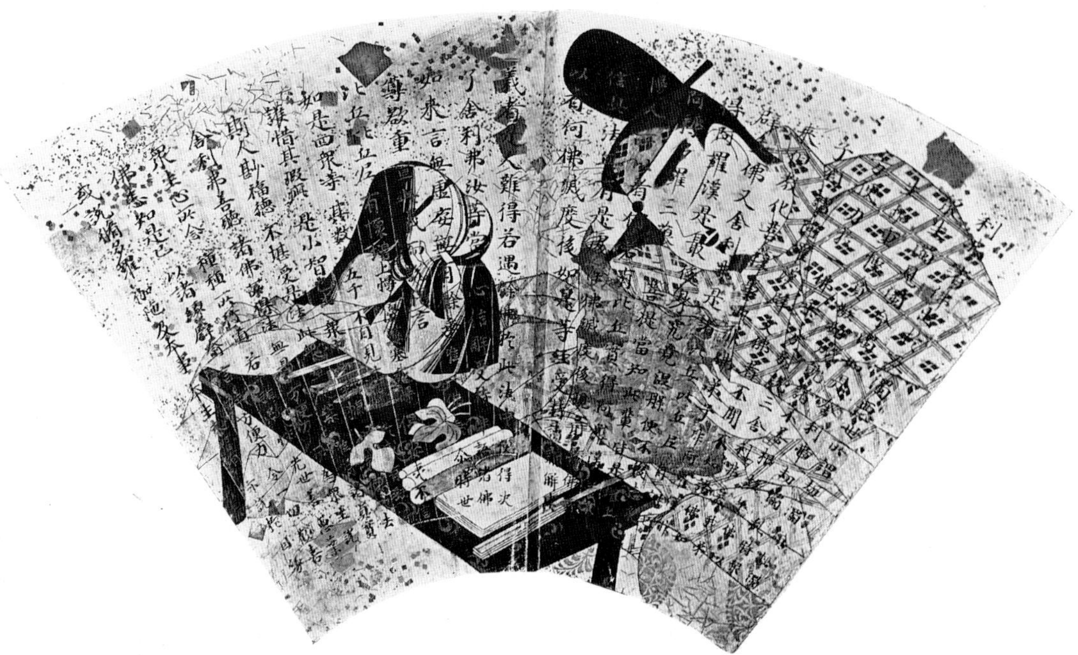

Figure 1 *Buddhist Sutra Fan*, dated 1188, woodblock design on paper with hand coloring and inscription, collection Shitenno-ji, Osaka.

viewer experiences when opening the fan from right to left. These three qualities of curvature, radiation, and movement are the characteristic compositional elements of the horizontal fan.

The earliest Japanese literary reference to fans is in the *Manyōshū* (an anthology of Japanese poetry written in the 8th century), which confirmed that the folding cypress fan was already present in Japan at that time. In the 1950's, a cypress fan with a painted monochrome ink surface was found in one of the arms of a Thousand Armed Kannon, one of the Buddhist sculptures in Kyoto's Tōji temple. This fan had been an offering to the temple in A.D. 877, and is thus the oldest verifiable painted cypress fan in Japan.

During the Heian period (794-1185), fans were first inscribed with Buddhist sutra scriptures. Later, figure compositions were wood block printed onto the fan surface, over which the scriptures and color were brushed by hand, creating objects of lasting beauty. Although this fan type was prevalent during the Heian period, unfortunately few remain. Those that survived were preserved as religious objects in temples, such as Shitenno-ji in Osaka and Hōryū-ji in Nara, and date to the 12th century. These examples are beautiful and graceful, depicting scenes from the lives of the nobility of the period (figure 1). Further documentation of fans exists in the historical and literary annals of the period. Lady Murasaki, author of the renowned 11th century *Tale of Genji,* commented that the court nobles held fans while ceremoniously waiting for the birth of an imperial child. At that time, the fan was associated primarily with the elegance of the aristocracy. In later centuries, the fan became more popular, accessible to and consequently used by greater numbers of people from all walks of life. No datable examples of fan

painting exist from the Kamakura period (1185-1333), although, presumably, large numbers of fans were produced and used at that time. Several lacquer stationary boxes produced during the Kamakura period are decorated in gold with designs of fans. Handscrolls of the same date also depict scenes of people using fans.

During the Muromachi period (1334-1573), an era of feudal society, fans were used ceremonially at court as well as for gifts on special occasions and the New Year. The impact of Chinese Zen Buddhism, paramount throughout Japanese society during this era, influenced Japanese painting. The Chinese Zen aesthetic included a simple, inconspicuous use of monochrome ink rather than color. This was in direct opposition to the grace and decorative characteristics of Japanese painting from the earlier four centuries of the Heian period. The result of this Chinese Zen influence was a sense of austerity and *shibui* (understated elegance) in monochrome ink painting (figure 2).

Japanese screens *(byōbu)* displaying fan paintings also have survived, beginning from the 15th-16th centuries. In the late 15th century, paper fans were ingeniously mounted on gold screens with the ribs hand drawn in ink or color. Occasionally, water patterns also were painted onto the surfaces of the screens, creating "screens of floating fans." Such painting is said to have been inspired by an old Kyoto story in which a youth accompanying a Shōgun's procession through Kyoto inadvertently dropped his fan from the bridge into the Saga River. Blown by the wind, the fan floated down the river creating a vivid scene which inspired all the other attendants of the Shōgun likewise to hurl their fans into the flowing waters. Screens of fans continued to be created by artists of the Rimpa tradition during the Edo period. Sōtatsu, Hōitsu, Kiitsu, and Hōchū produced beautiful compositions by painting fans directly onto the screen, arranging them in aesthetically satisfying but visually complex ways.

During the 16th century, a family of painters known as Kanō, who also were influenced by Chinese taste, produced the majority of fan paintings in studios much like the craft guilds of medieval Europe. Generally, these painters directly transferred their subject matter from the horizontal and vertical formats of hand and hanging scrolls onto the fan surface without inventing new design solutions for the unique shape of the fan. The vast majority of Kanō fans were produced for utilitarian purposes by workshops and rarely obtained the grace and skillful compositional designs that became evident in the 17th and 18th centuries with the individual creative painters of the Rimpa and Nanga schools.

In the early 17th century, painting workshops were thriving in the prosperous cities where anonymous "town painters" (artists working in these shops) supplied the demands of the everyday citizen by mass producing fans and other artworks. These "town painters" evolved from both the Kanō tradition and the native Japanese decorative school which had originated in the Heian period (*yamato-e* style). Many fans depicting city scenes were produced, as were fans for a game called *Kemari* and for Nō plays. Moreover, fan paintings for the tea ceremony, which had developed in the Muromachi period, became popular.

The Edo period (1615-1868), Japan's greatest era of widespread artistic creativity,

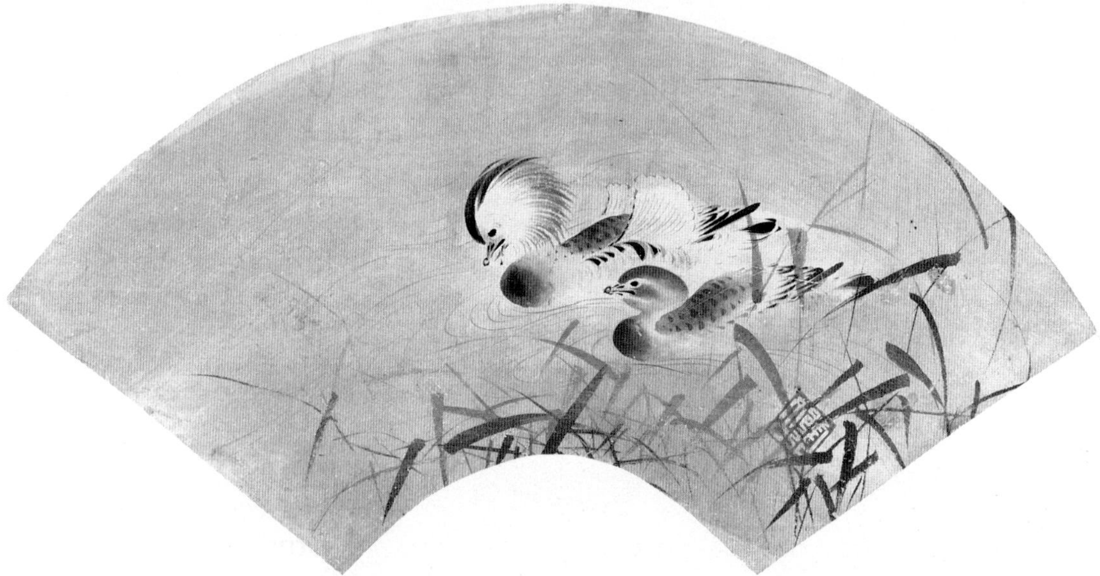

Figure 2   Shikibu (Ryūkyō), active mid-16th century, *Ducks and Reeds*, ink on paper, collection Harry G. C. Packard.

witnessed a tremendous production of fan paintings by a host of artists representing the many schools of art that flourished at that time. During this period, the fan was used by all levels of society, as well as in the theatre for Nō and Kabuki performances. Scholars, poets, and philosophers employed the fan for self-expression and for copying classical literature and poetry. Fans were often presented as gifts or as tokens of esteem, a custom that survives to this day. Many artists inscribed fans with poetry prior to presenting them to friends as a symbol of good feelings. The many Edo fans that have survived in fine condition attest to the fact that, even during their era of creation, these objects were highly admired and collected.

During the past 150-200 years, collectors assembled fan paintings into albums, either all by a single artist or by a number of different painters, ensuring their preservation in pristine condition. Sometimes, fan paintings were remounted onto screens combined with large and small album leaf paintings. These album leaves were square or rectangular and, although more conventional in shape than the fan, shared in its intimacy of size, resulting in interesting overall screen compositions.

All of the fans in this publication were painted during the Edo period (1615-1868), when many new schools of painting evolved and flourished. In no other period has any society matched the volume or the diverse creative energy seen during this time. Japanese fan painting likewise reached its zenith then, as many of the great masters enjoyed this format for both its creative and design potential.

During the Edo period, Japan was closed to outside foreign influence and trade and a 260 year hiatus of relative peace endured. Japanese society underwent dramatic changes in structure. The warrior class of samurai declined in significance, while the emerging merchant class, who congregated in Tokyo, Kyoto and Osaka, prospered. Under the rule of the Tokugawa Shōguns, the capital of Japan was moved to Edo (now Tokyo), where the population rapidly grew to more than one million. Cultural changes took place in large part because of a new system of education, based on Confucian ideology, which dramatically increased the literacy rate. Cultural appreciation of art, music, theatre and poetry became more widespread, particularly among the large number of city dwellers and the increasingly important mercantile community.

The combination of peace, prosperity, lack of foreign influence, and changes in cultural and economic conditions produced an aesthetic environment which allowed Japanese painters the freedom to express themselves. This variety of artistic expressions was incorporated into many schools of art including Shijō, Nanga, Rimpa, Ukiyo-e, Zenga, Nagasaki and others. The diverse patronage of the many schools of art reflected the eclectic tastes of a changing society. The Shōgun government in the capital of Edo continued to patronize the traditional, Chinese inspired, Kanō school; whereas the wealthy nobility appreciated the more beautiful and decorative Rimpa style. The merchant classes of the Kansai region (Kyoto-Osaka) favored the naturalistic styles of the Maruyama-Shijō schools; whereas the Tokyo mercantile community became enamored with Ukiyo-e artists, who depicted subjects of the "Floating world" of courtesans and their society. The Imperial Court, which remained in Kyoto, favored the more traditional Japanese narrative style *(yamato-e)*, which was continued through the Edo period by artists of the Tosa school. Zen paintings were produced by Buddhist monks who, inspired by Zen enlightenment, generally painted as a means of self expression or as a teaching tool for their students and patrons. The Zen painters were predominantly patronized by the numerous temples of Japan and, interestingly, rarely painted in the fan format.

This tremendous outpouring of creative talent over a 250 year period, coming from within the structure of the individual schools of painting and from unaffiliated, eccentric artists, was unmatched in any other period of Japanese art, and perhaps any other period in Eastern or Western art history. Of the great number of fan paintings produced during the Edo period, perhaps the most innovative and creative works were executed by artists of the Rimpa, Nanga, and Shijō schools, which constitute the subject of this selection.

RIMPA-SCHOOL OF DECORATIVE PAINTING

Rimpa, the decorative school of Japanese art, began in the early 17th century and was characterized by the use of bold, intense color and design. This school of painting, considered uniquely Japanese with little or no foreign influence, has, in the past fifty years, been deeply appreciated by both Westerners and the Japanese.

Rimpa painters employed new techniques of applying ink or color onto the still wet surface of a painting *(tarashikomi)*, creating a subtle, natural and succulent appearance. The visual effect of *tarashikomi* was to create a surface textural quality previously unknown in Japanese painting. Rimpa artists were especially creative and skillful in painting on fans. They fully utilized the elements of the radiating lines, upper and lower borders, and movement to create interesting and vital landscape, bird and flower, and figure paintings in this format. Their abilities in both horizontal folding fans and round fans were among the important achievements of the Rimpa school.

Tawaraya Sōtatsu, who worked in the first half of the 17th century, was the pioneer of the decorative style and is considered a master of fan painting. Firm attributions to him are limited and it is probable that the majority of early Rimpa fans attributed to his hand were school works made at his fan shop in Kyoto by his assistants or later followers. Nevertheless, his importance as a fan painter is primary to the development of this art form. His reputation rests on his bold color designs and individualized compositions in the horizontal fan format. His great screen masterpieces, designated national treasures in Japan, are described by the art historian, Hiroshi Mizuo, as having their basis in the compositional techniques that he developed while painting on fan-shaped surfaces.

Sōtatsu's sense of design, composition, and use of rich, deep color, without surrounding outlines, were outstanding. He freely transformed complex scenes from famous Japanese handscrolls of earlier periods into fan paintings. Much like a blowup of a photograph, he highlighted details of complex scenes which effectively produced creative and energetic images (figure 3).

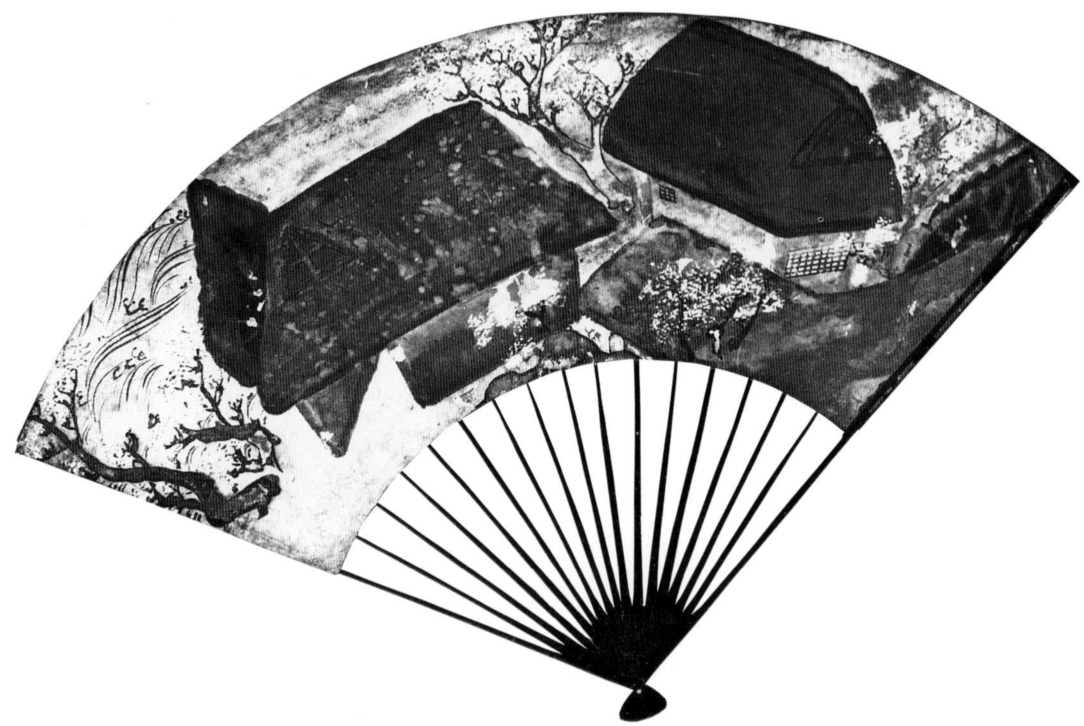

Figure 3 Tawaraya Sōtatsu (flourished first half of 17th century), *Farmhouses in Spring,* ink and color on paper, collection Sambō-in, Daigo-ji, Kyoto.

The Rimpa tradition further developed with the more stylized, rigorous, and sharply painted works of Ogata Kōrin (1658-1716). This artist's works combined the influence of traditional ink painting (Kanō school), with forceful abstract design in bold color and strong line. Although he excelled in all fan types, he favored the round fan *(uchiwa)*. These circular fans were mounted on lightweight thin handles which, with gentle finger rotation, permitted successive viewing of the front and back surfaces of the fan. Kōrin painted both surfaces, harmonizing pictorial designs on the two sides into skillfully blended compositions. Over the years, many of these fans were dismantled from their original form and mounted as individual hanging scrolls. This explains the appearance of unsigned works by Kōrin, since often only one side of the fan was signed or sealed by the artist.

Sakai Hōitsu (1761-1828), who came from a noble family and was himself quite wealthy, continued the Kōrin tradition with virtue, elegance, and refinement, using the most brilliant and beautiful colors available. He excelled in traditional folding fan designs and had a broad scope of painting abilities ranging from flower and grasses to animals, birds and figure paintings.

Nakamura Hōchū (flourished 1790-1818), who lived in Osaka, was a contemporary of Hōitsu. His painting technique, more rustic and less refined than Hōitsu's, avoided the use of boundary lines and was most original and bold. His fan paintings demonstrate the use of *tarashikomi* and *tamekomi* (the absorption of color and ink

back into the brush from the painting surface) to their fullest extent. In his fan paintings he brilliantly merged intentional artistic design with the indeterminate character and effect of *tarashikomi.* Hōchū's effortless command of the *tarashikomi* puddling technique, coupled with his adroit and skillful use of the fan shape as a painting surface, makes him one of the most important fan painters of the Edo period. Like Sōtatsu, his ability to magnify images into significant detail in the horizontal fan format showed exceptional skill and daring originality.

Suzuki Kiitsu (1796-1858), Hōitsu's student and successor, continued the Rimpa tradition until the end of the Edo period, when the vitality and vigor of Rimpa art waned. He excelled in detailed, original compositions and the use of hard-edge, opaque color and continued the refined painting tradition of Hōitsu.

NANGA SCHOOL

Many of the folding fans of the Edo period were produced by the literati or Nanga artists, who particularly favored the challenge of this format. These artists were often poet-painters and amateurs in contrast to the mostly professional painters of the Kanō, Shijō, Tosa and Rimpa schools. The literati group was characterized by great individuality and freedom of expression. They painted a wide range of subjects, including birds and flowers, fish, Zen subjects, and pure calligraphy, but concentrated on landscapes. This group of artists, who often were friends, frequently held gatherings at which they shared the Japanese concept of the "virtues of a scholar"—namely, enjoying a gathering that focuses on poetry, calligraphy, music and painting. Many of these artists are known for their great love of nature and their predilection for saké. Often, they would present each other with paintings (including fans) as tokens of friendship, and would inscribe poems onto each others' works as symbols of shared creativity and comradeship. The expressions of the great literati artists, such as Taiga, Buson, Gyokudō, Kazan, Bunchō and others, demonstrate their innovative, clearly recognizable and distinctive styles.

Nanga artists were originally inspired by Chinese painting, which was mostly studied second hand in woodblock painting manuals, such as *The Mustard Seed Garden,* an influential book imported into Japan from China in the 16th and 17th centuries. These woodblock printed books described detailed methods and techniques of how to paint rocks, mountains, still lifes, flowers, bamboo, etc. Although the pioneer Nanga artists studied these manuals, they were able to transform such stereotyped painting techniques into brilliant forms of individual self-expression.

Fan paintings created by Nanga artists differed from those efforts produced in large numbers by "town painters" and professional Rimpa painters. The primary concern of the Nanga artist was to display his individuality in its purest form on the fan surface. These artists were not always vitally concerned with the compositional details of the fan format and showed great variation in their ability to successfully adapt to the arched curvature of the fan. Nanga artists, in general, were not as preoccupied with the sale of their work or the presence or absence of supporting patrons. Their paintings were executed mostly for their creative enjoyment.

The pointillist-like style developed by the Ike Taiga (1723-1776) and his followers is one of the great achievements of Japanese art of the 18th and early 19th centuries, predating the scientific pointillism of Seurat and the Neo-Impressionists in France by more than 100 years. Taiga was particularly gifted as a fan painter, a talent recognized early in life when as a teenager he opened a fan shop in Kyoto. He is represented in this publication by both his colorful pointillistic landscapes and his more cursive, poignant and simple ink paintings of landscape and orchid.

Yosa Buson (1716-1784), another of the Nanga masters, is represented by two examples of landscape and figure fan painting incorporating haiku poems (17 syllable poems unique to Japan) based on the tradition of Bashō (1644-1694), the most distinguished haiku poet in Japan.

Uragami Gyokudō (1745-1820) was a true literatus who enjoyed music, saké and travel, as did many of the other Nanga painters. His energetically drawn *sumi* ink brush strokes produced mystifying and spirited landscapes, unparalleled by his contemporaries. Gyokudō, along with Taiga and Buson, skillfully combined his individual self-expression in painting with considerable agility in using the curvature and radiance of the horizontal fan format.

Other excellent examples of Nanga landscape are found in the fan paintings by Kō Fuyō, Kinkoku, Bunchō, Bōsai, Baiitsu, Chikutō, Gyokuran, Gyokushū, Hankō, Beisanjin and Kaikai. Excellent Nanga fan paintings of bamboo, orchid, and figures by Taiga, Kazan, Gyokuran, Chinzan and Baitei also were included in this volume.

MARUYAMA-SHIJŌ SCHOOLS

In the late 18th century, two new painting schools emerged that catered to the tastes of the merchants of Kyoto, a class that was then gaining status and power. The Maruyama school was founded by Maruyama Ōkyo (1733-1795), who combined earlier painting traditions, particularly Kanō, with a new interest in Western techniques and a study of nature. Branching off from the Maruyama school was the Shijō school, originated by Matsumura Goshun (1752-1811), who studied first with the Nanga master Buson and then with Ōkyo. These two schools were characterized by a strong sense of realism, the use of light wash colors, and a more gentle feeling than the highly self-expressive Nanga artists.

By the 18th and 19th centuries, the fan had become such a universal object in Japanese society that all painters worked in this format at one time or another. Nevertheless, it appears that the prominent Maruyama and Shijō painters only occasionally employed the fan format in contrast to the Nanga and Rimpa masters; consequently, relatively few fans by these artists exist. Furthermore, few of these artists were particularly recognized for their ability as fan painters, in contrast to Sōtatsu and other Rimpa masters whose fan paintings were paramount in their oeuvre. Notwithstanding, fine examples of these softer, naturalistic-realistic schools can be seen and are included in the works of Nangaku, Rosetsu, Gitō and Zeshin.

Rosetsu (1754-1799), although originally a student of Ōkyo, later became a highly individual and eccentric painter and is now considered a major pioneer of self-expression during the Edo period. The dragon and landscape fans in this volume demonstrate his imaginative, lively and uninhibited expressions, which differed markedly from the more controlled idealistic manner of Ōkyo.

Shibata Zeshin (1807-1891), one of the most well known Shijō painters and lacquerers, is represented here by two works. The circular-shaped landscape fan is an excellent example of his superb landscape style employing lacquer as the medium of expression. The inspiring fan album of bird and insect paintings by Zeshin also merits recognition as an outstanding Shijō work, incorporating compositional excellence in the horizontal fan format.

The Meiji period (1868-1912) introduced mammoth changes into Japanese society, by virtue of the Westernization that immediately followed the reopening of the country to foreign trade and influence. After 1868, the creative energy of the flourishing schools of art of the Edo period declined and, with the exception of solitary artists of high individual achievement, such as Tessai, Rengetsu, Zeshin and others, stylization and uniformity resulted. Western influences predominated and although fan painting became a highly successful Japanese commercial export product, the artistic and creative quality of the earlier periods was lacking.

In summary, I have provided an overview of the entire history of Japanese fan paintings with particular reference to the Edo period. Although fan paintings represented only a small percentage of the total creative output of Japanese artists, they, nevertheless, provide valuable insights into the mood and talent of the era. Undaunted by uniformity in shape and configuration, Japanese fan paintings demonstrate the varied approaches and differing expressive capabilities of individual artists throughout the Edo period. This publication, rather than a pure scholarly text, is intended to share in the joy of creativity found in these works of art, and to provide the general Western audience with a more familiar background to enhance their perception and appreciation of Japanese fan paintings.

KURT A. GITTER, M.D.

LENDERS TO THE EXHIBITION

Art Gallery of Greater Victoria, *British Columbia*
The Ashmolean Museum, *Oxford*
The British Museum, *London*
The Brooklyn Museum
The Mary and Jackson Burke Collection, *New York*
William G. Clark, *Hanford, California*
The Cleveland Museum of Art
Kurt A. Gitter and Millie H. Gitter, *New Orleans*
Edwin Janss, *Thousand Oaks, California*
Mr. and Mrs. Leighton R. Longhi, *New York*
The Metropolitan Museum of Art, *New York*
Museum of Fine Arts, *Boston*
Cornelius and Shizuko Ouwehand-Kusunoki, *Zürich*
Sansō Collection, *United States*
Seattle Art Museum
Shin'enKan Collection, *United States*
Shōka Collection, *Lawrence, Kansas*
Mr. and Mrs. James Stein, *New York*

RIMPA

1 School of Tawaraya Sōtatsu, *Screen with Fan-shaped Paintings*

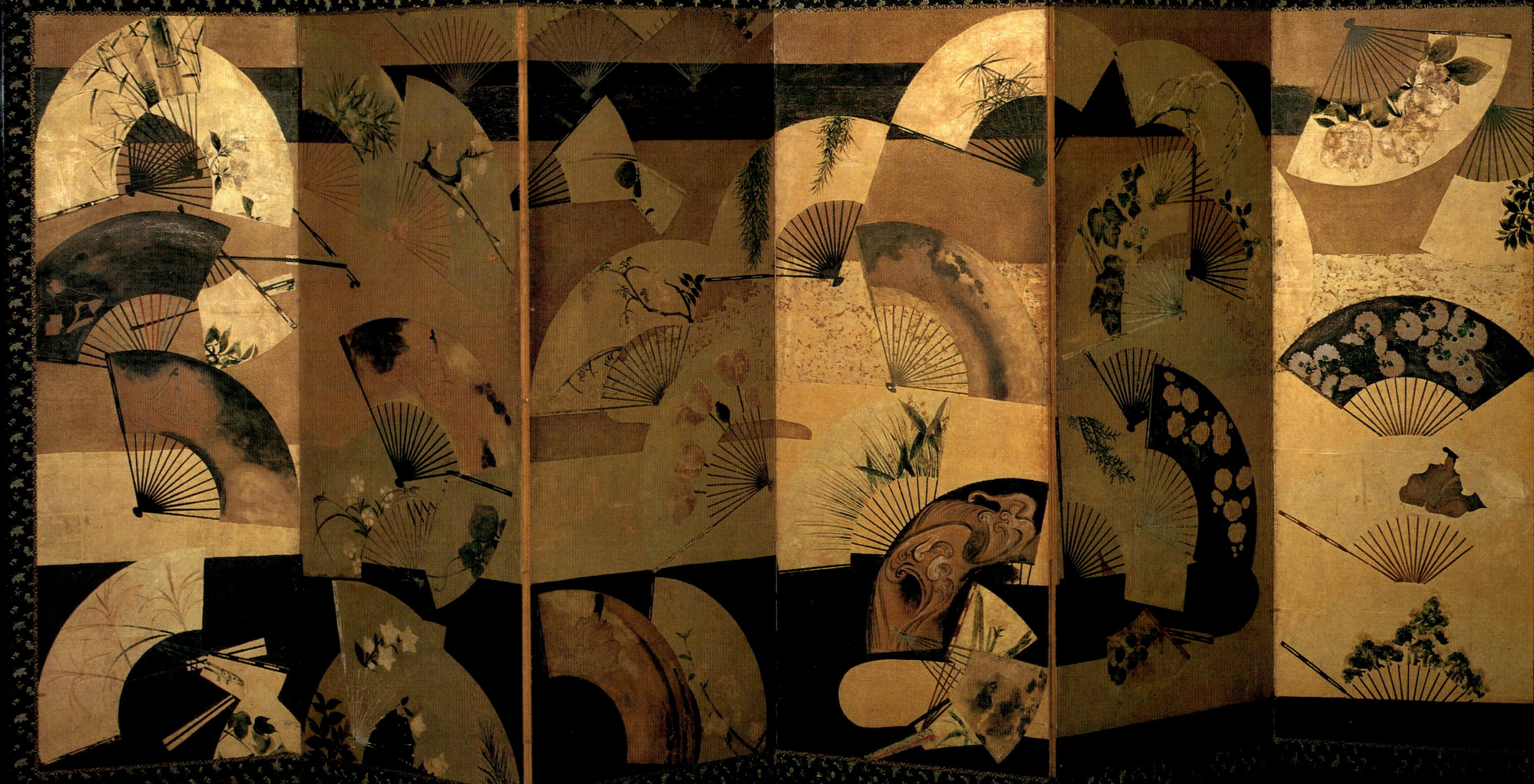

2   Ogata Kōrin, *Utsunoyama Scene from Tale of Ise*

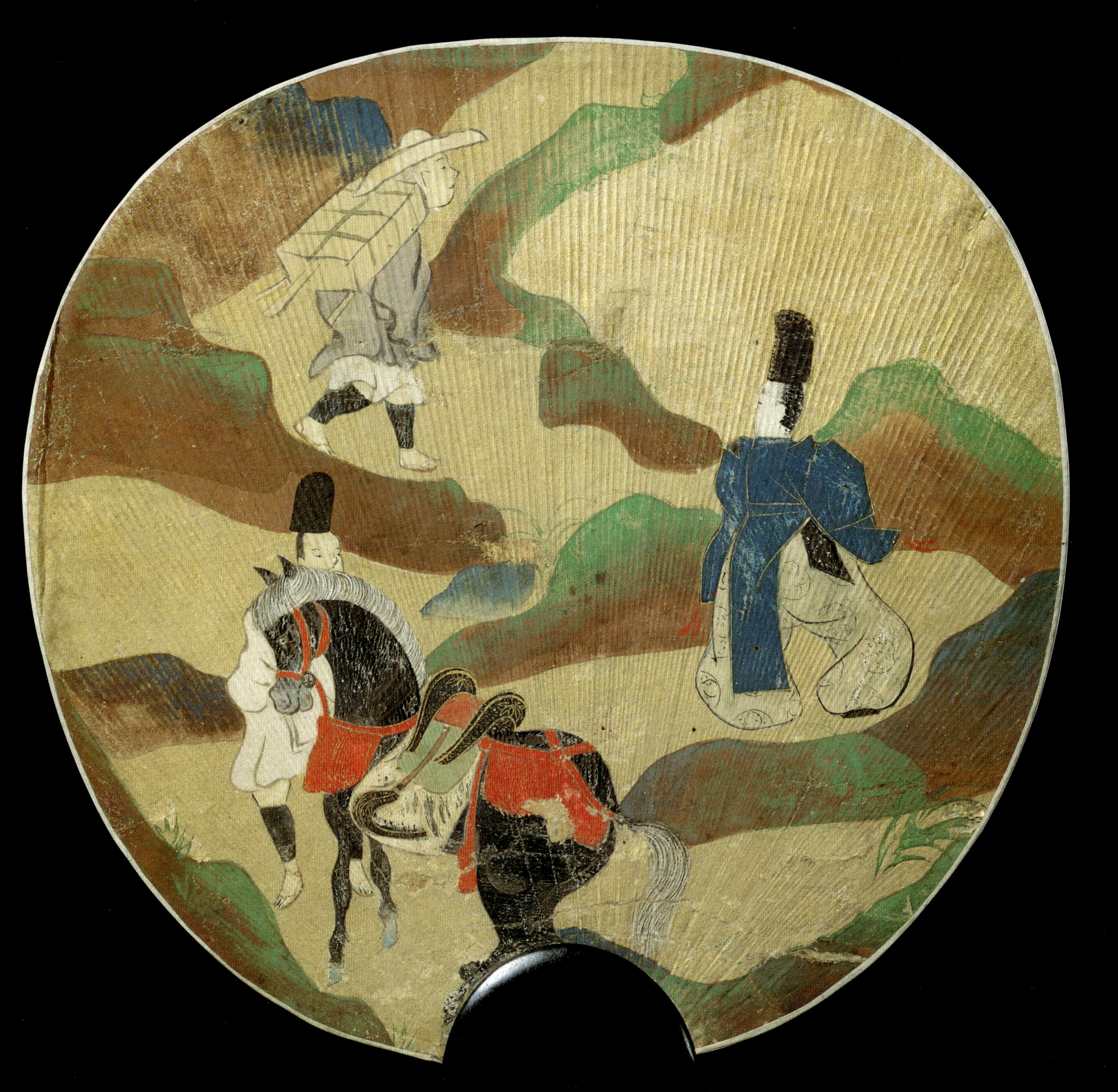

3   Ogata Kōrin, *Autumnal Ivy Leaves with Bamboo*

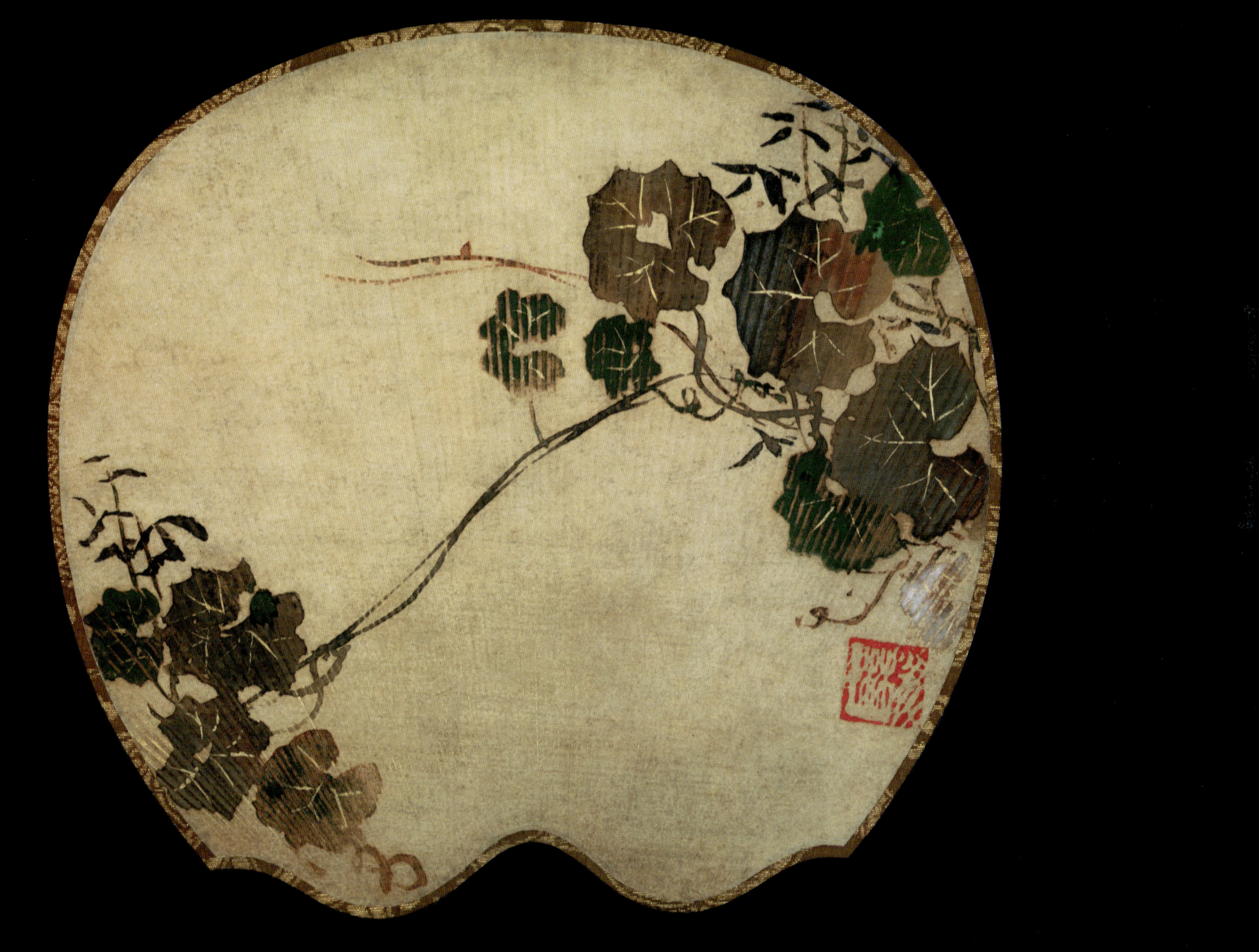

4   Ogata Kōrin, *Spider*

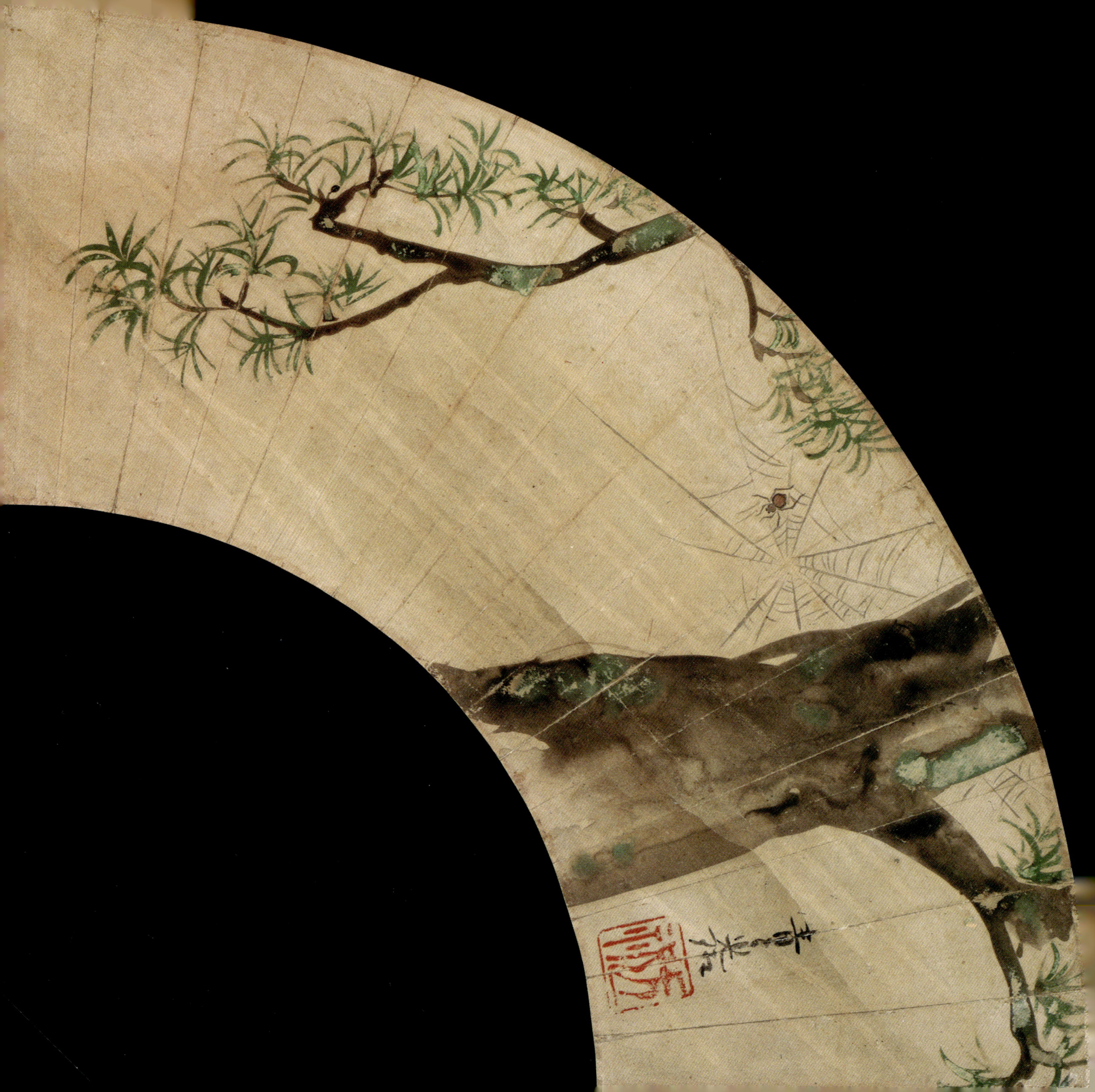

5   Ogata Kenzan, *Basket of Flowers and Grasses*

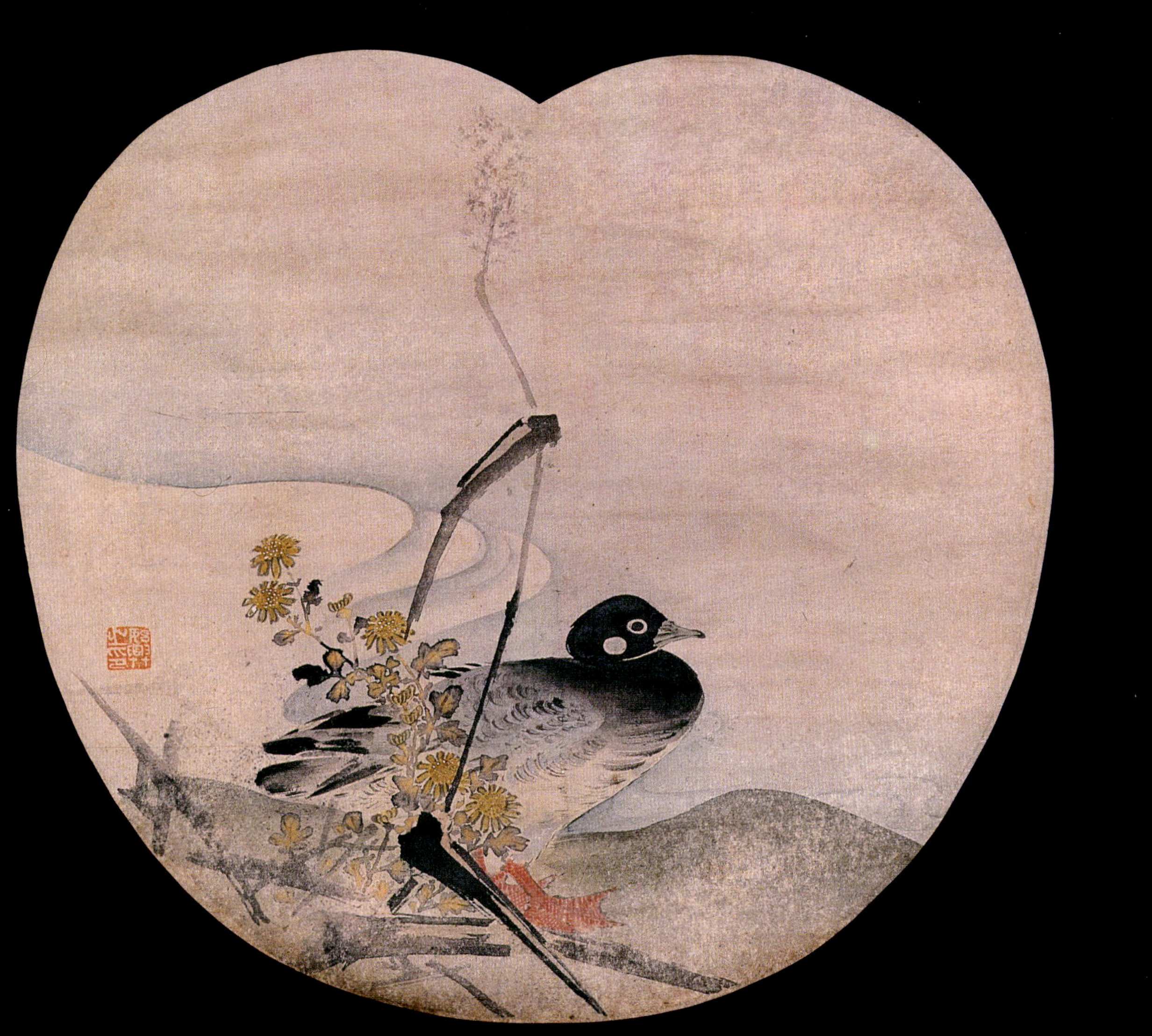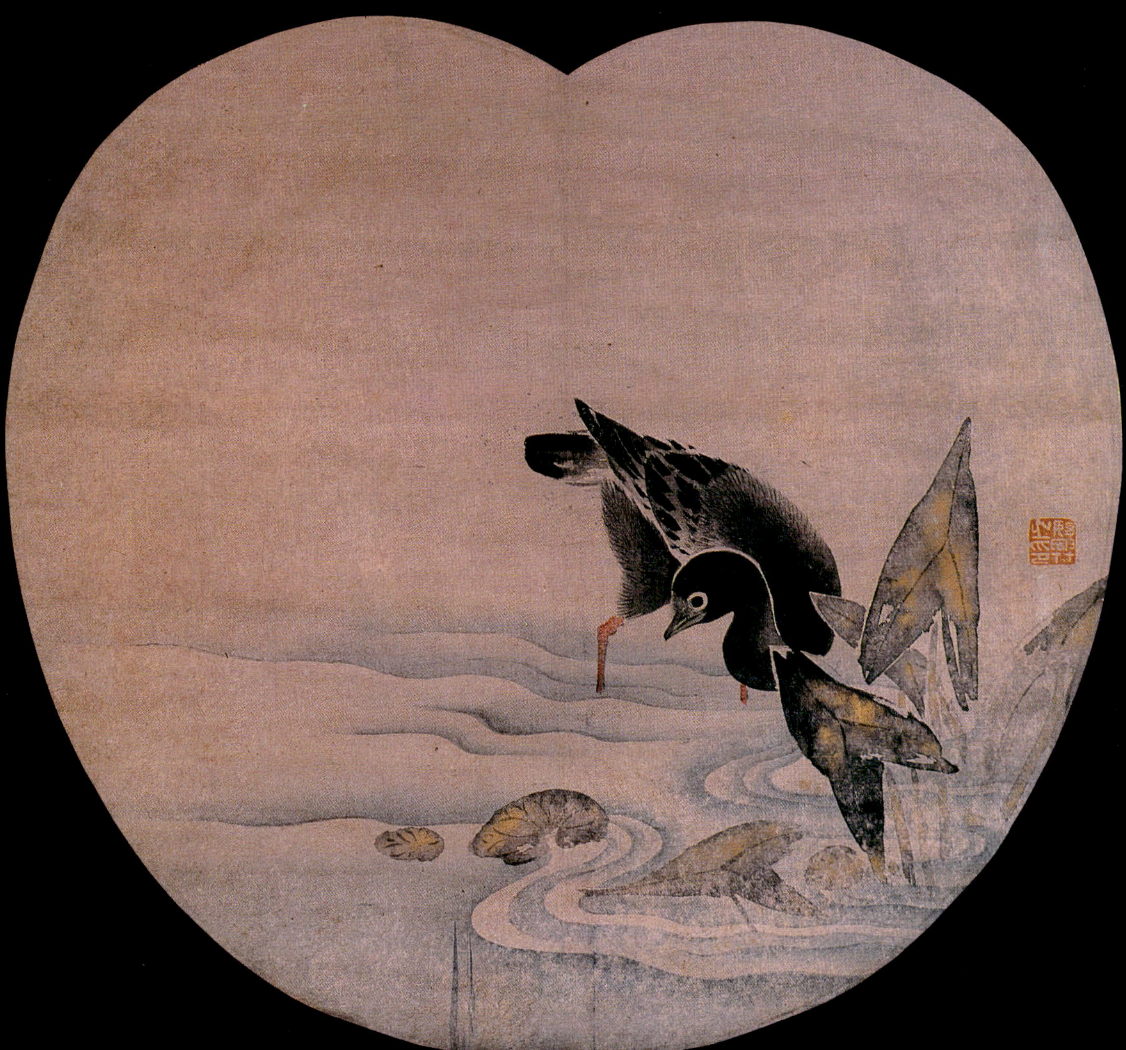

7   Attributed to Fukae Roshū, *Utsunoyama*

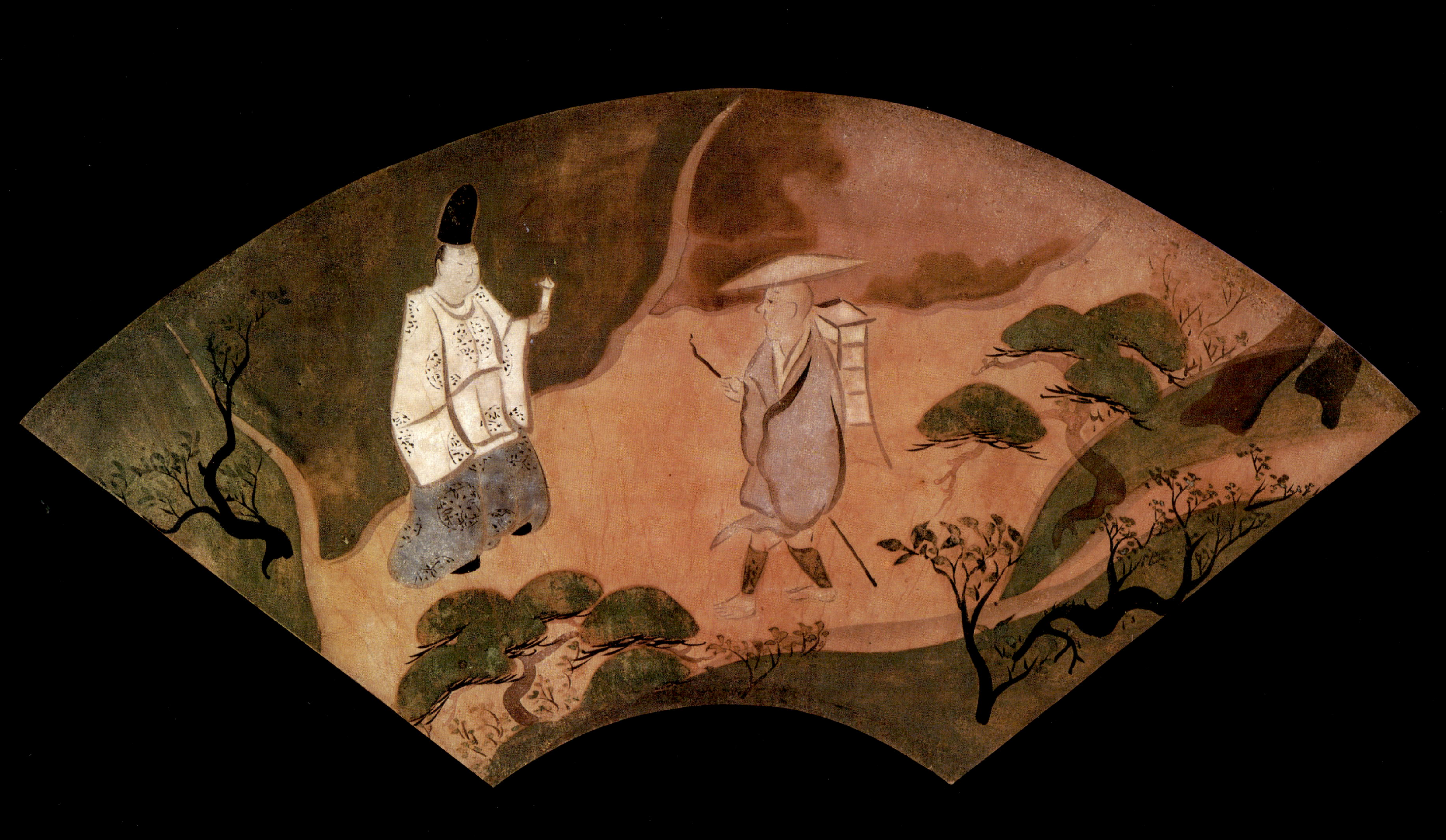

6   Watanabe Shikō, *Waterbirds*

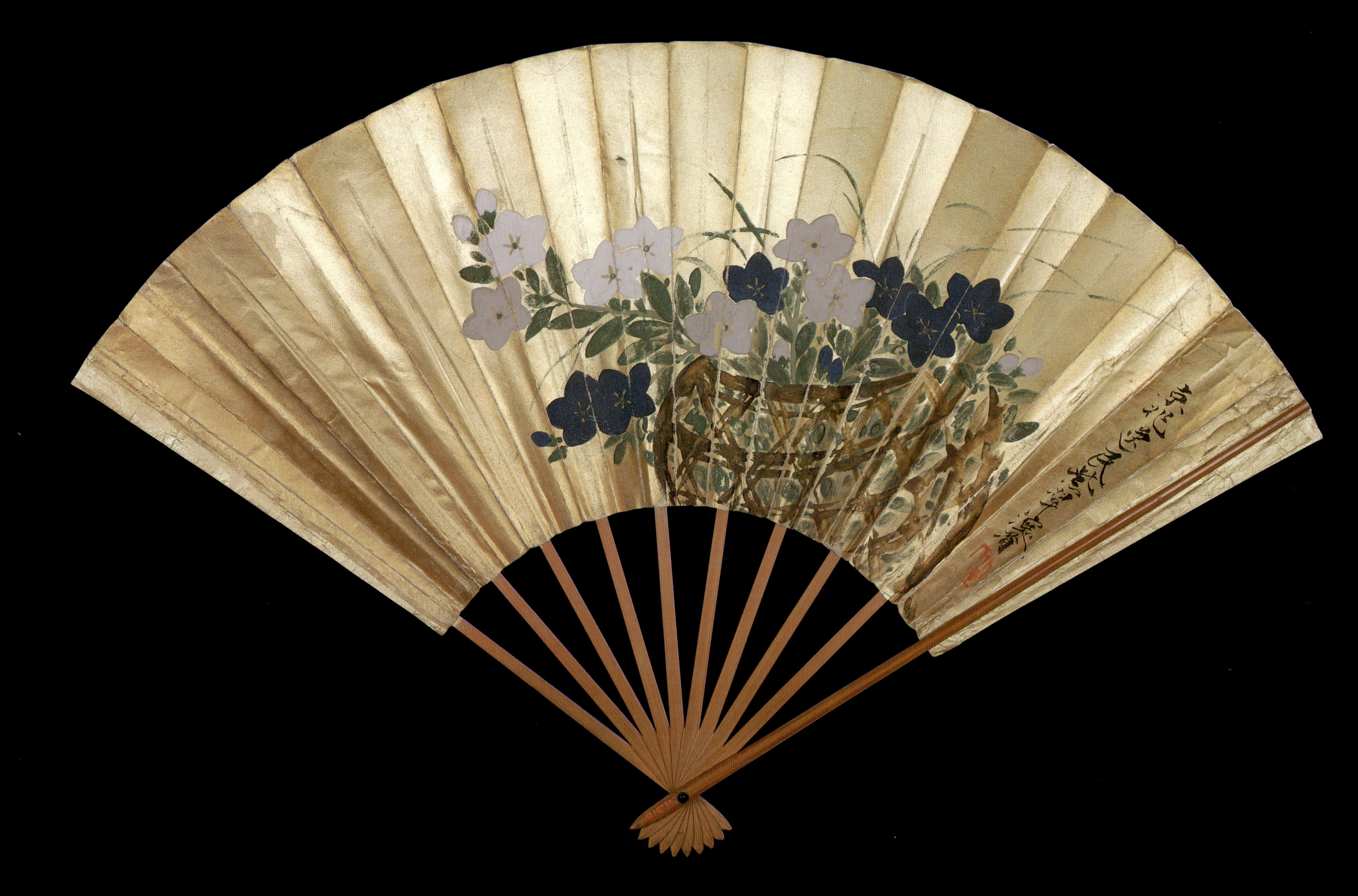

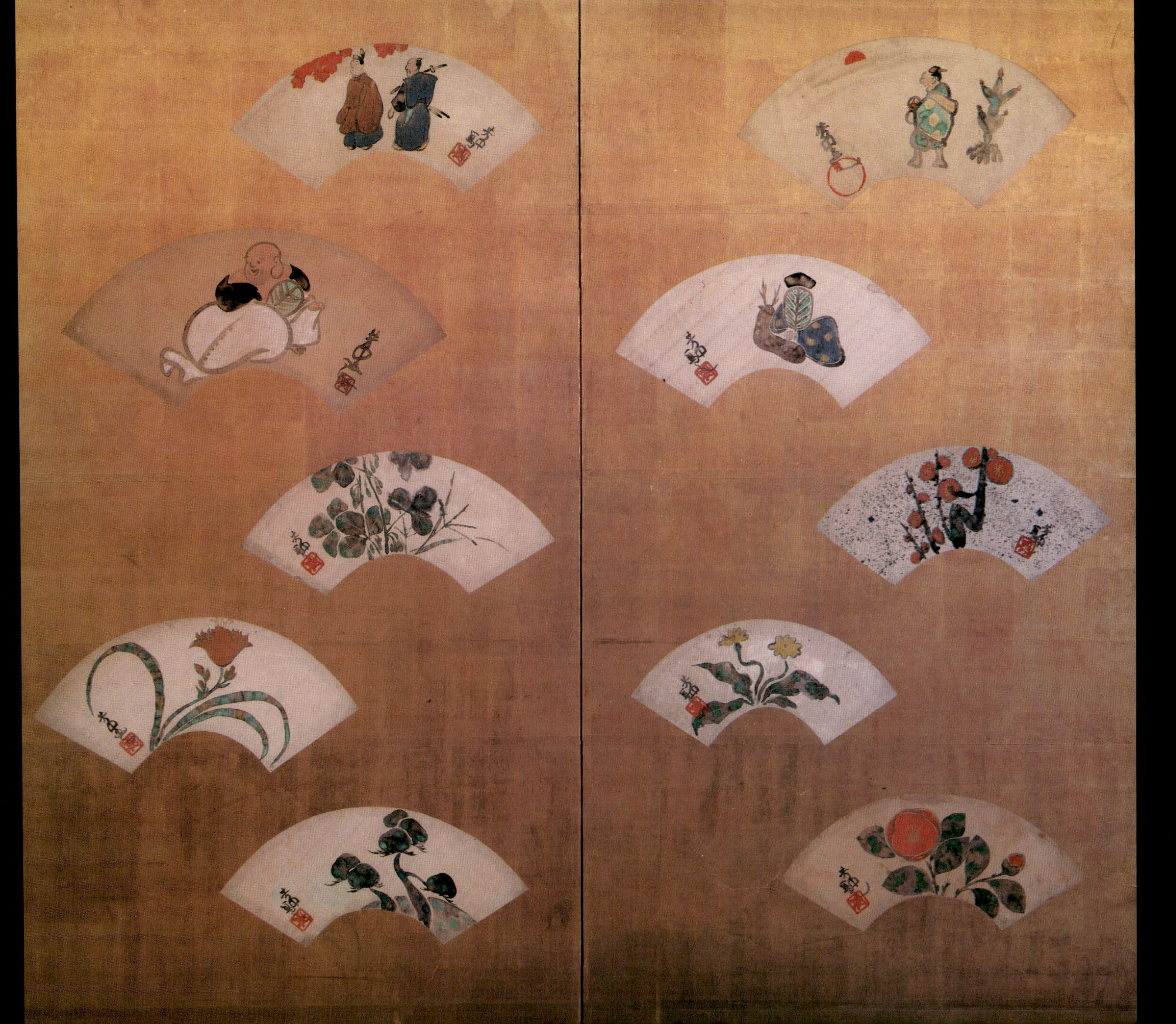

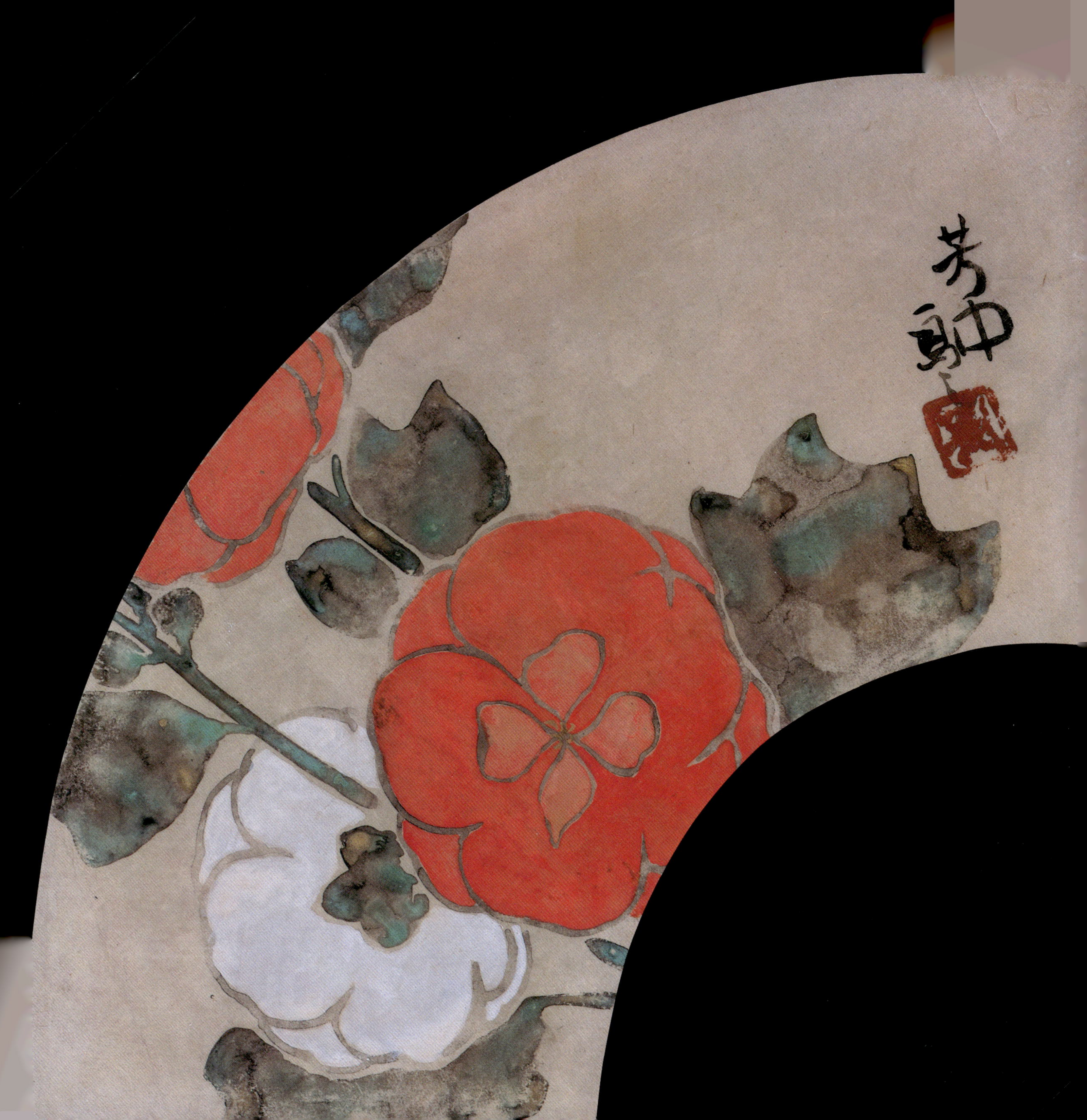

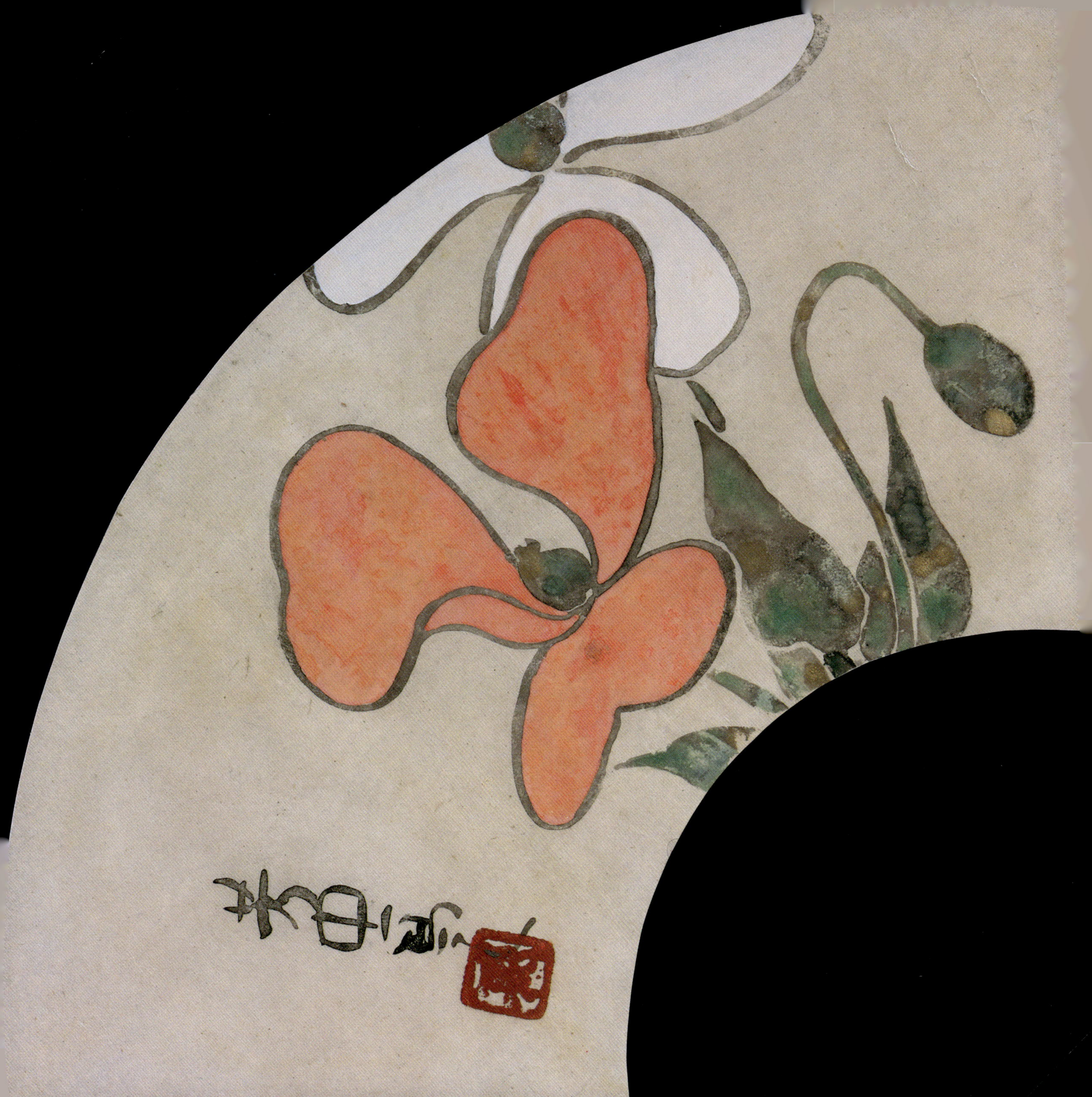

11   Nakamura Hōchū, *Gourd*

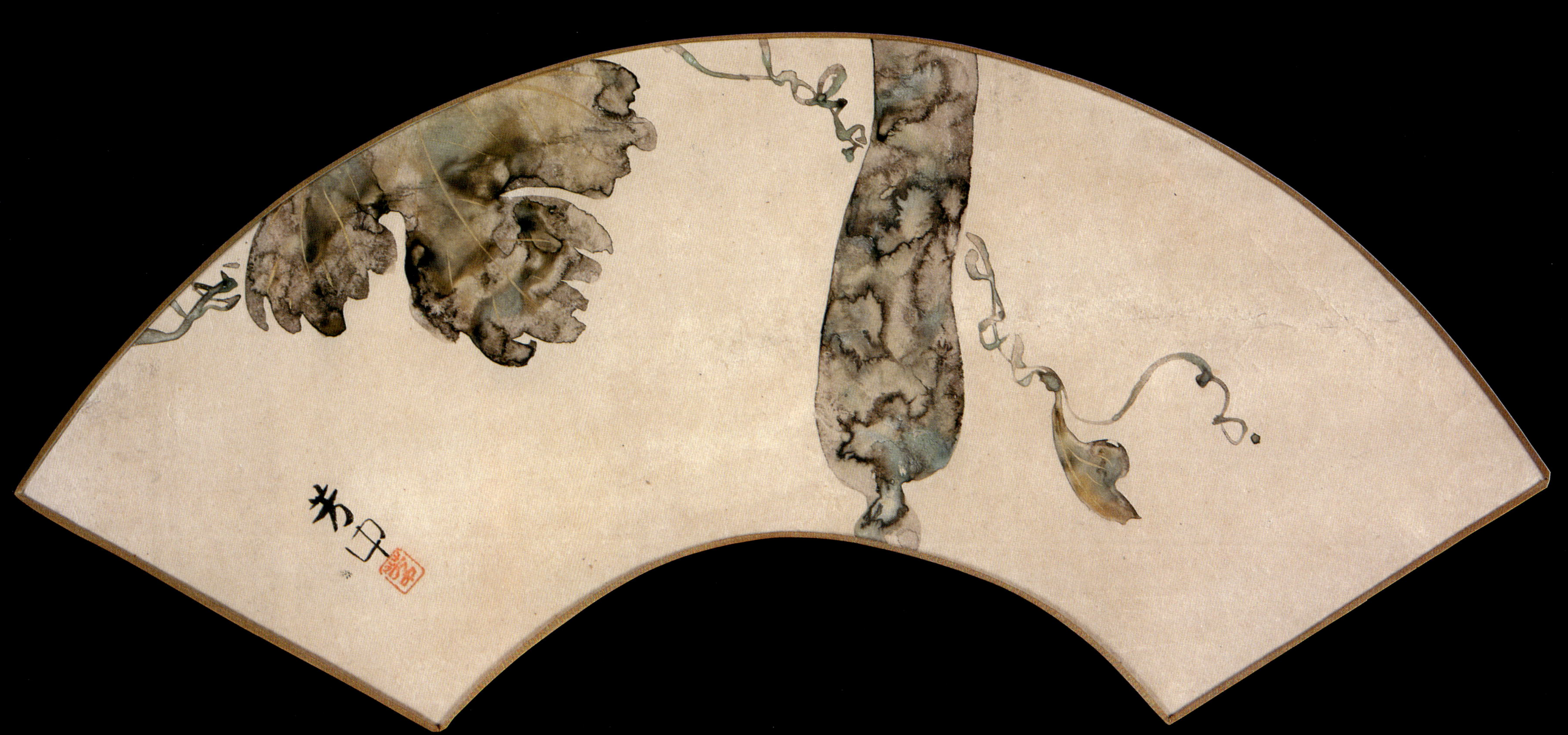

12   Nakamura Hōchū, *Crane*

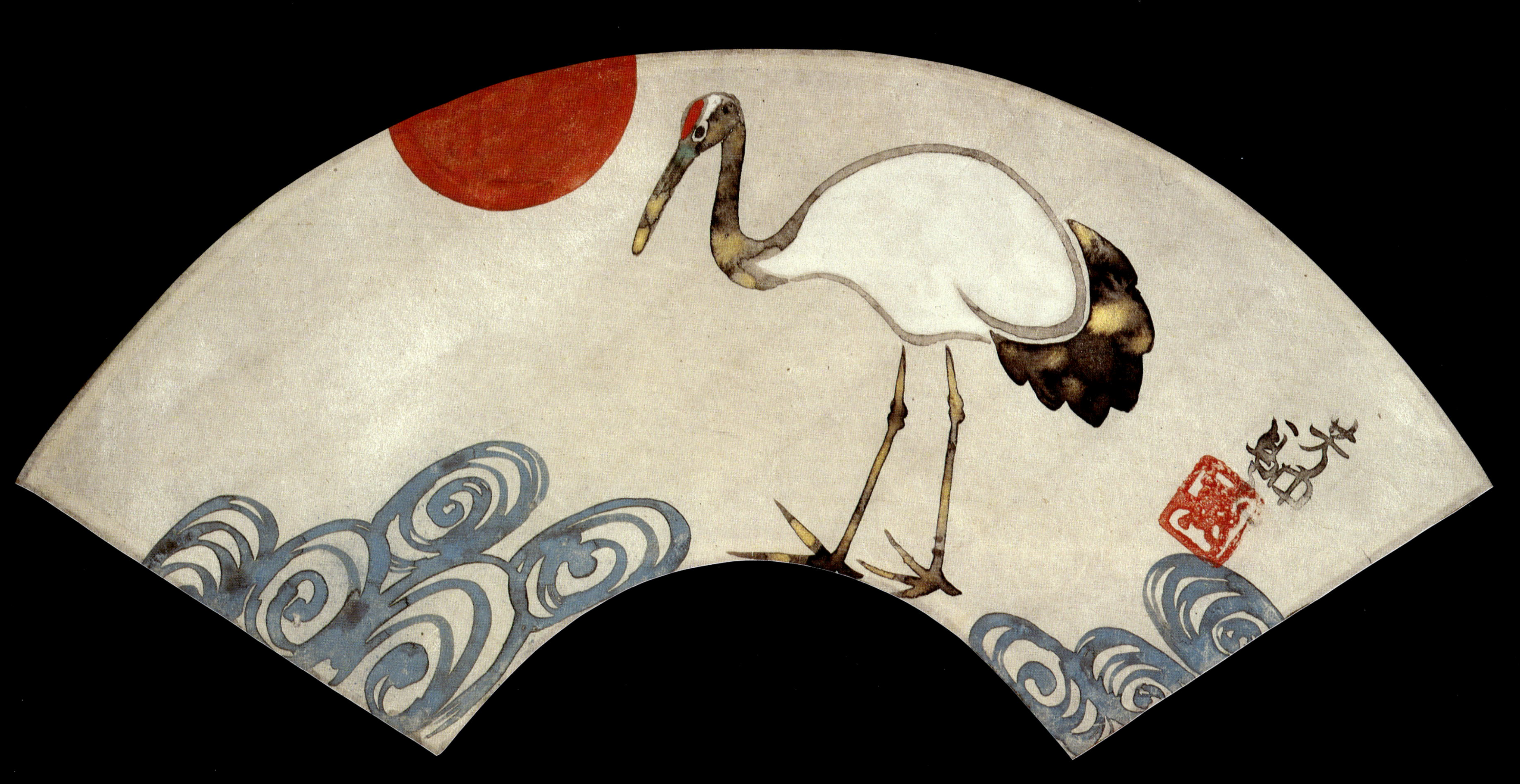

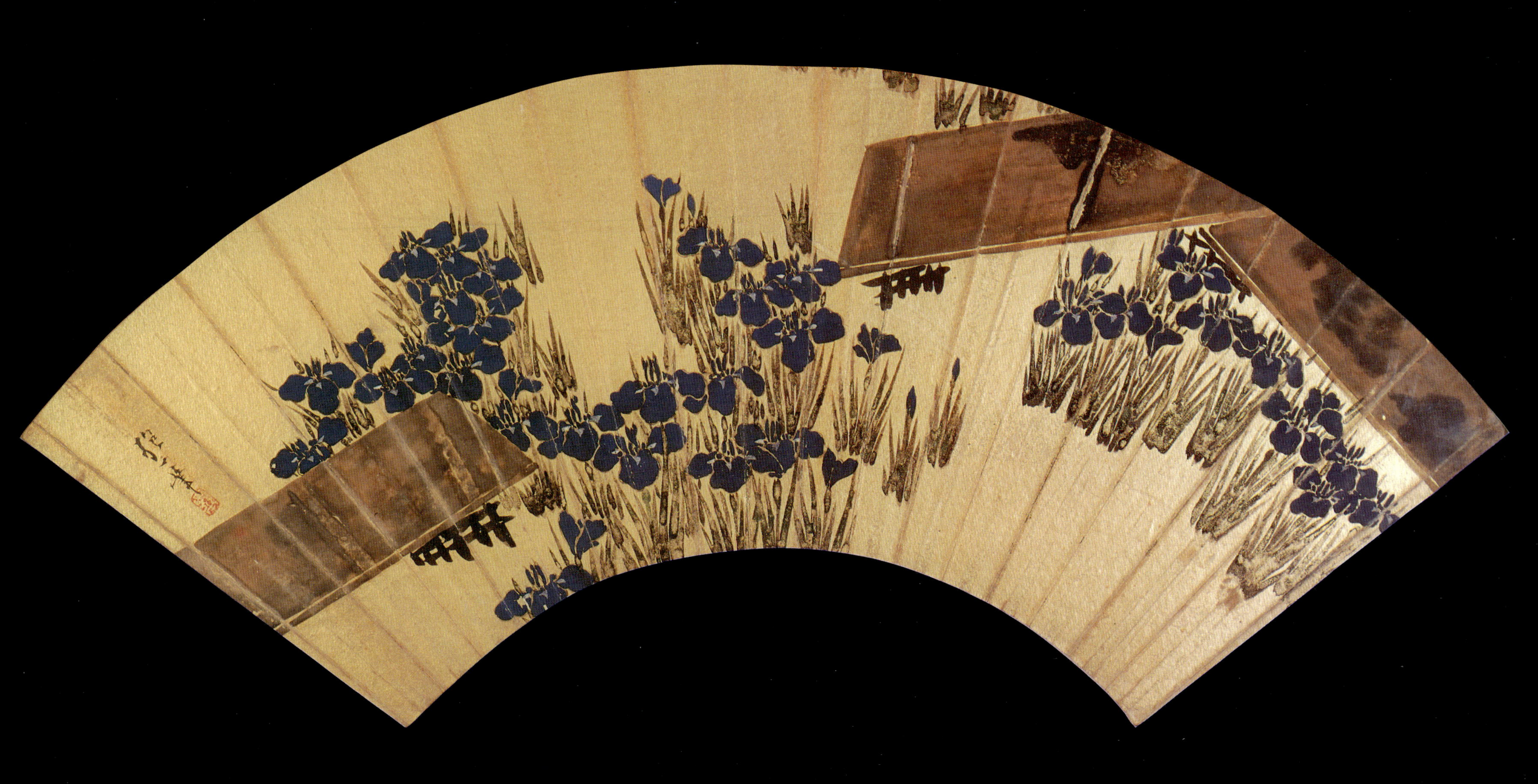

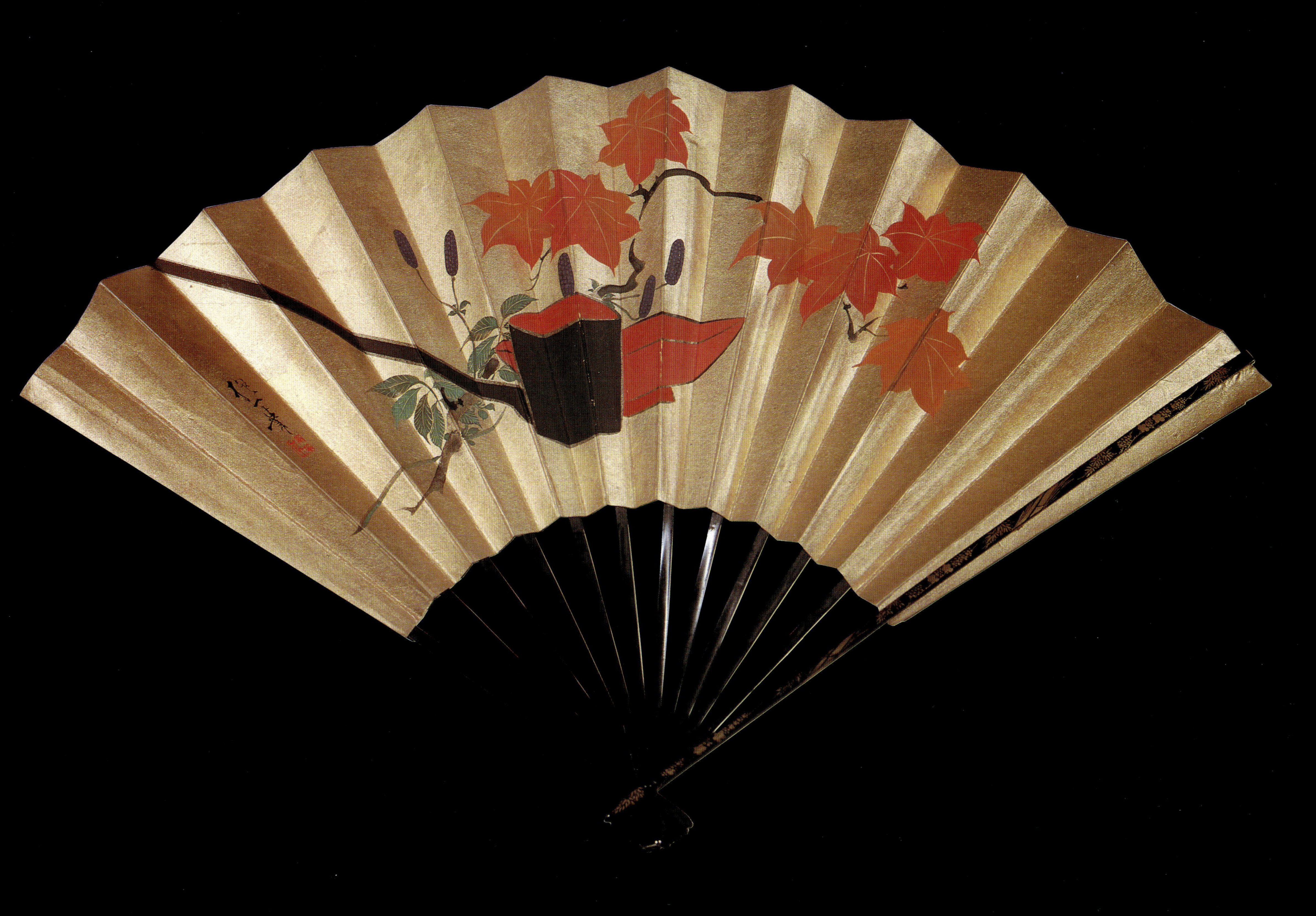

15   Suzuki Kiitsu, *Futami Bay*

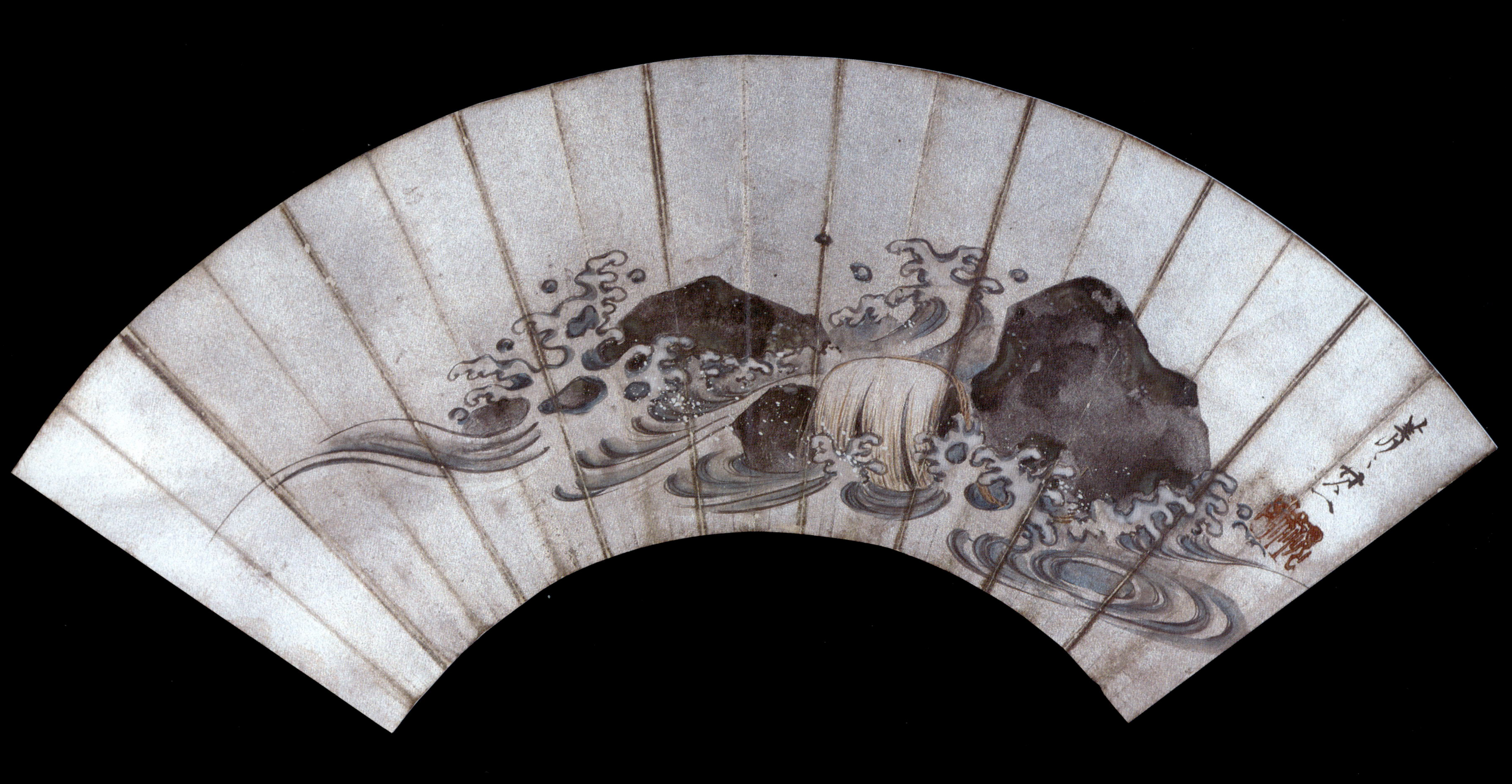

NANGA

16   Yosa Buson, *Narrow Road to the Deep North*

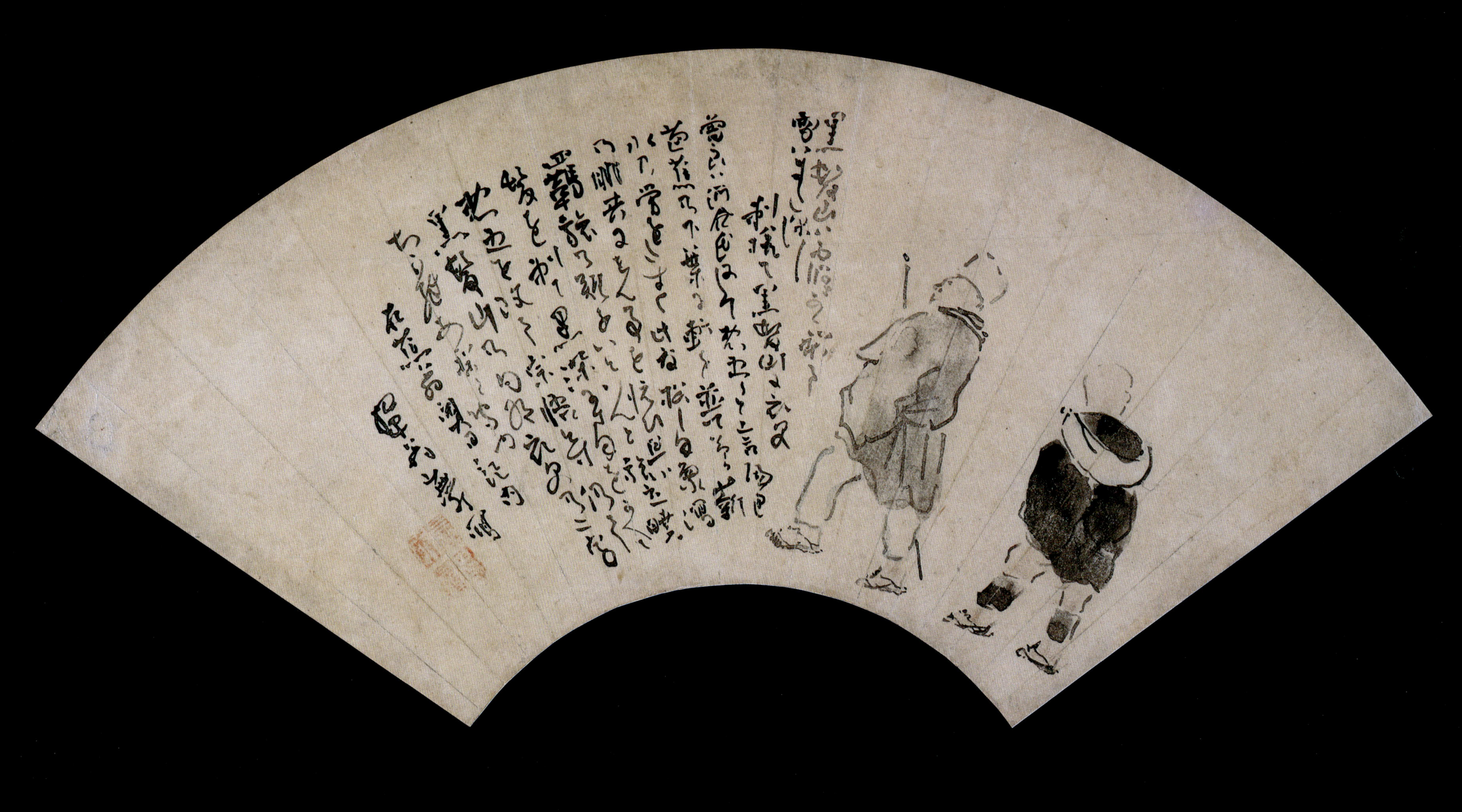

17   Yosa Buson, *Narrow Road to the Deep North*

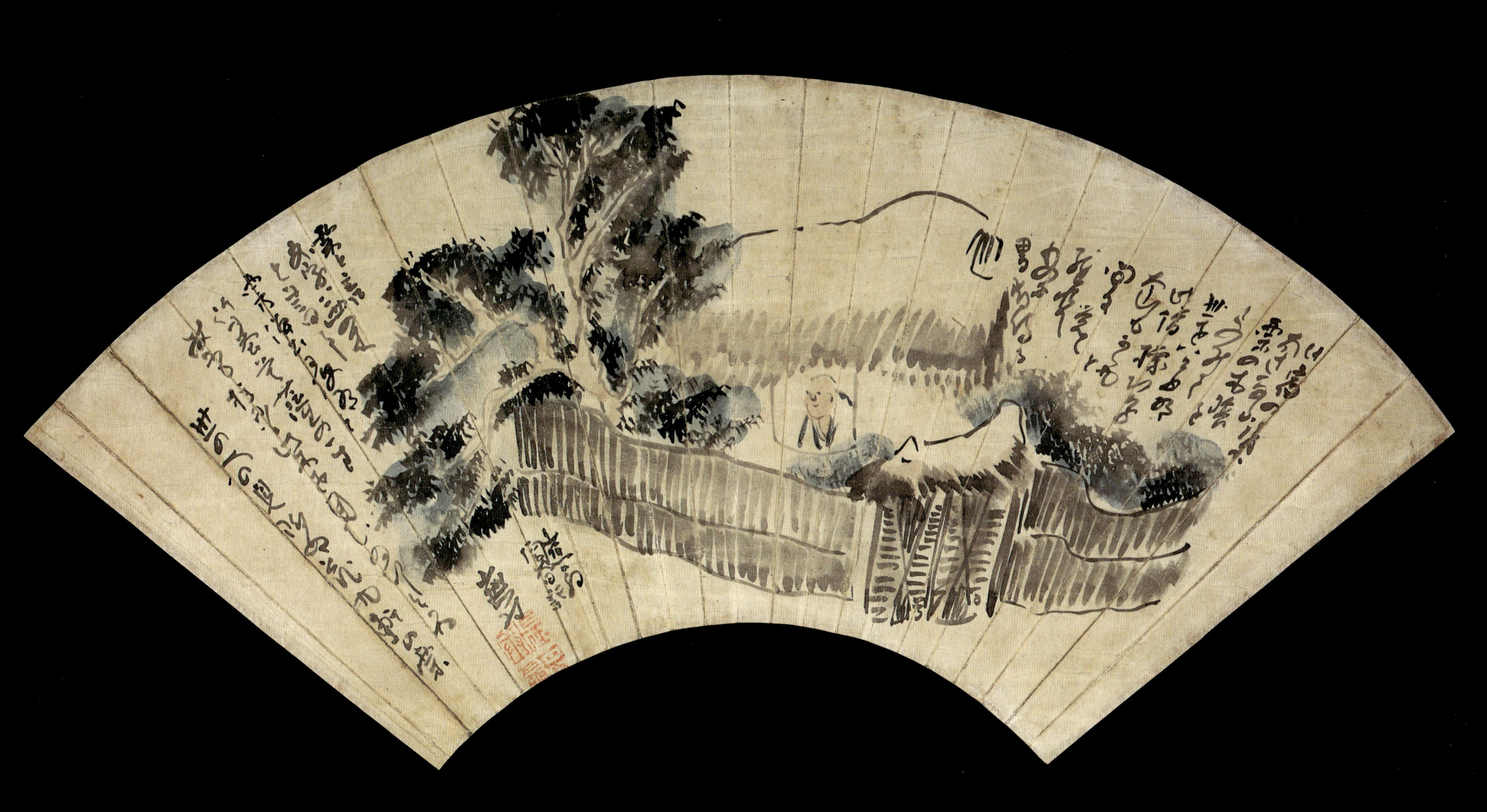

18   Kō Fuyō, *Landscape*

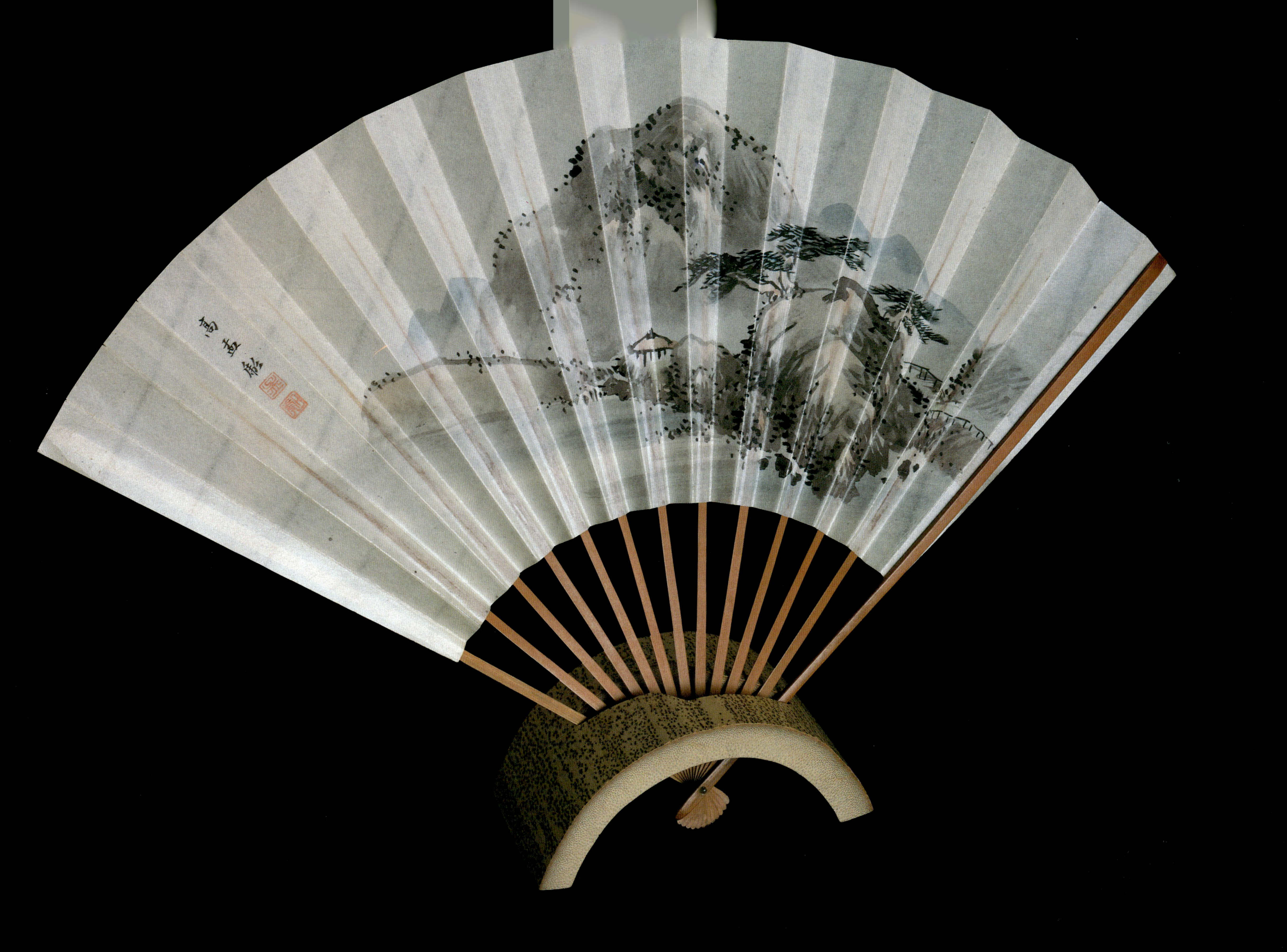

19   Ike Taiga, *Orchid*

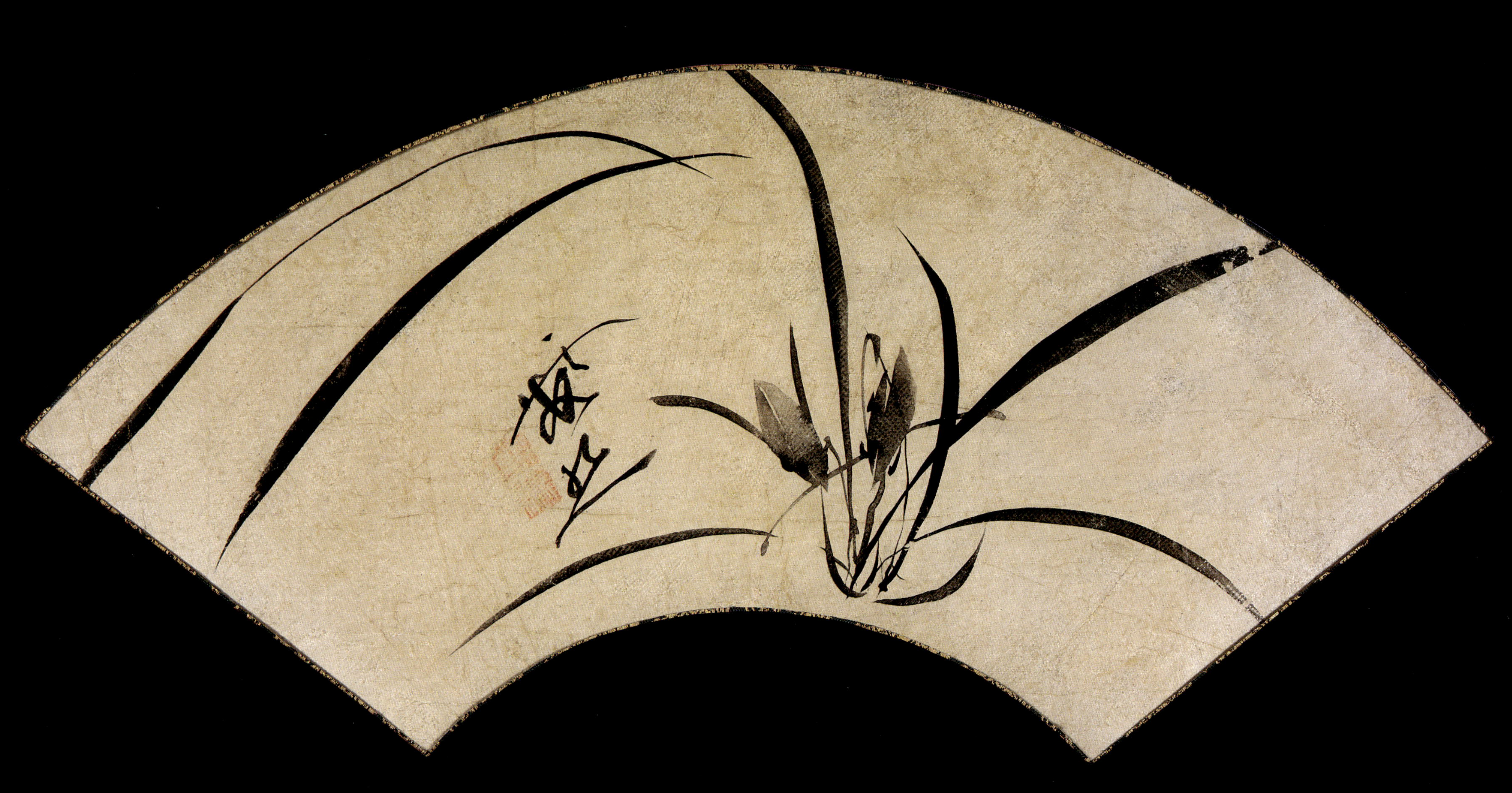

20   Ike Taiga, *Cultivating and Weeding the Fields*

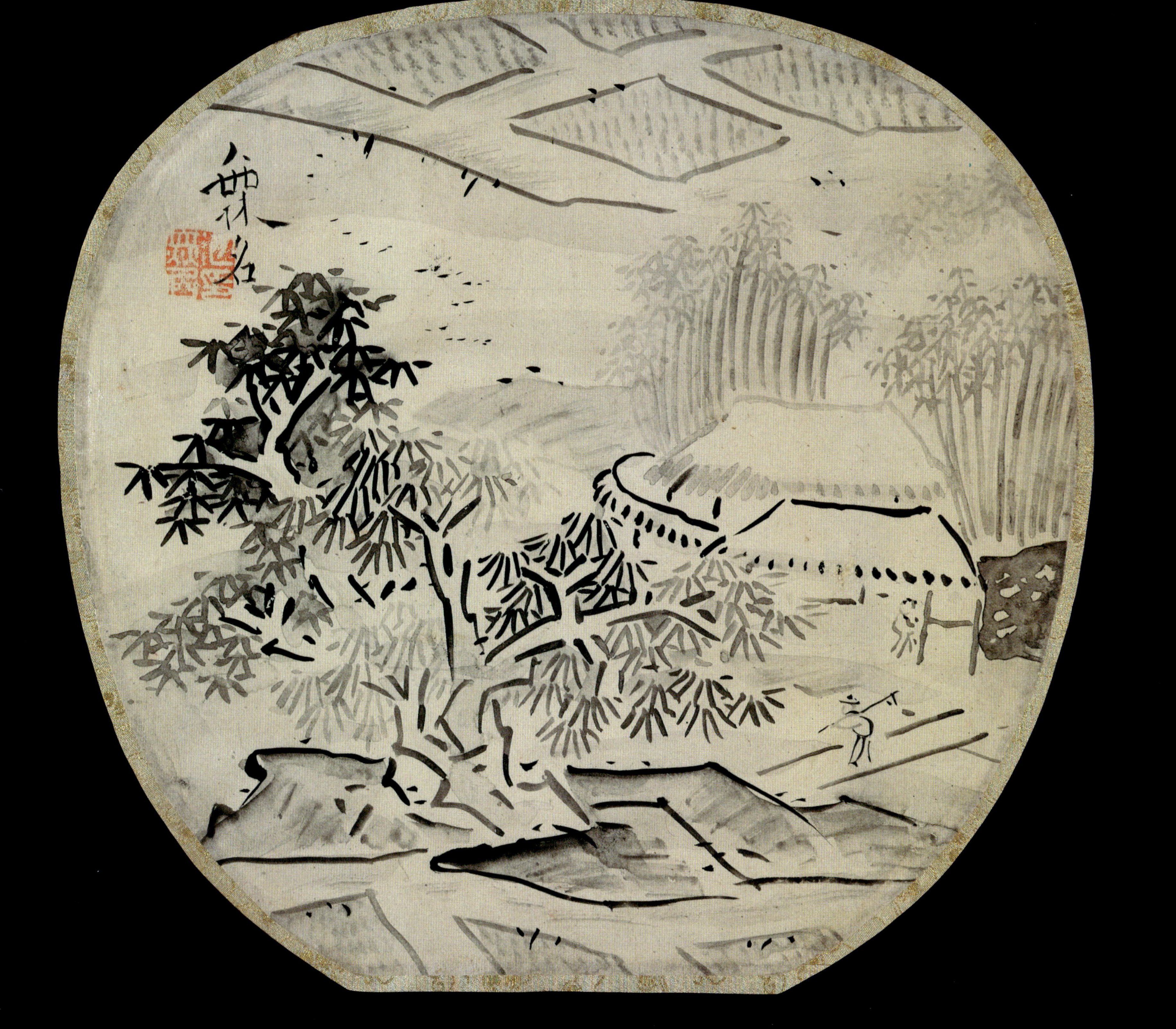

21   Ike Taiga, *Landscape with Yellow Trees*

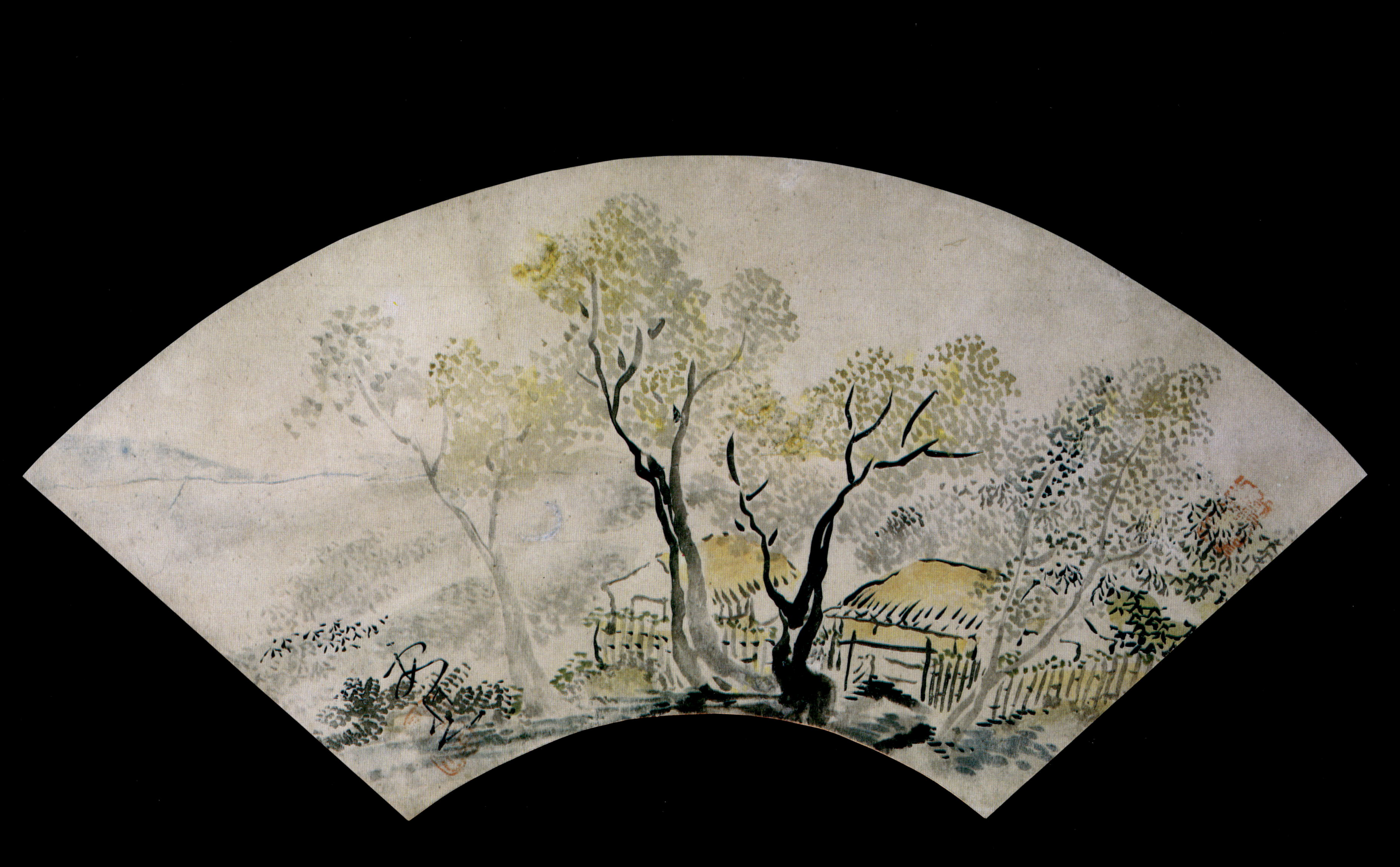

22   Ike Taiga, *Mount Fuji*

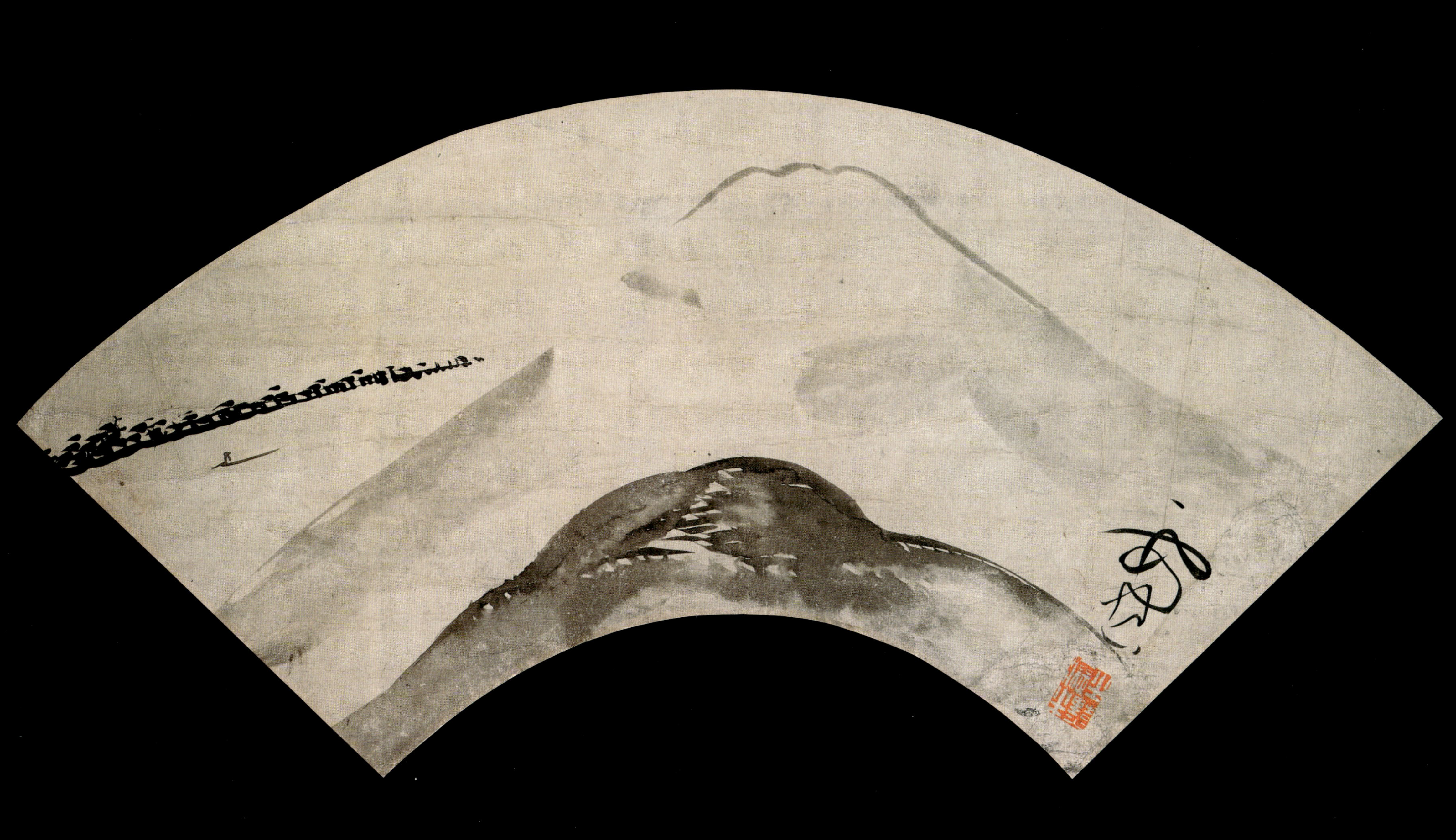

23   Ike Taiga, *Country Retreat in Early Summer*

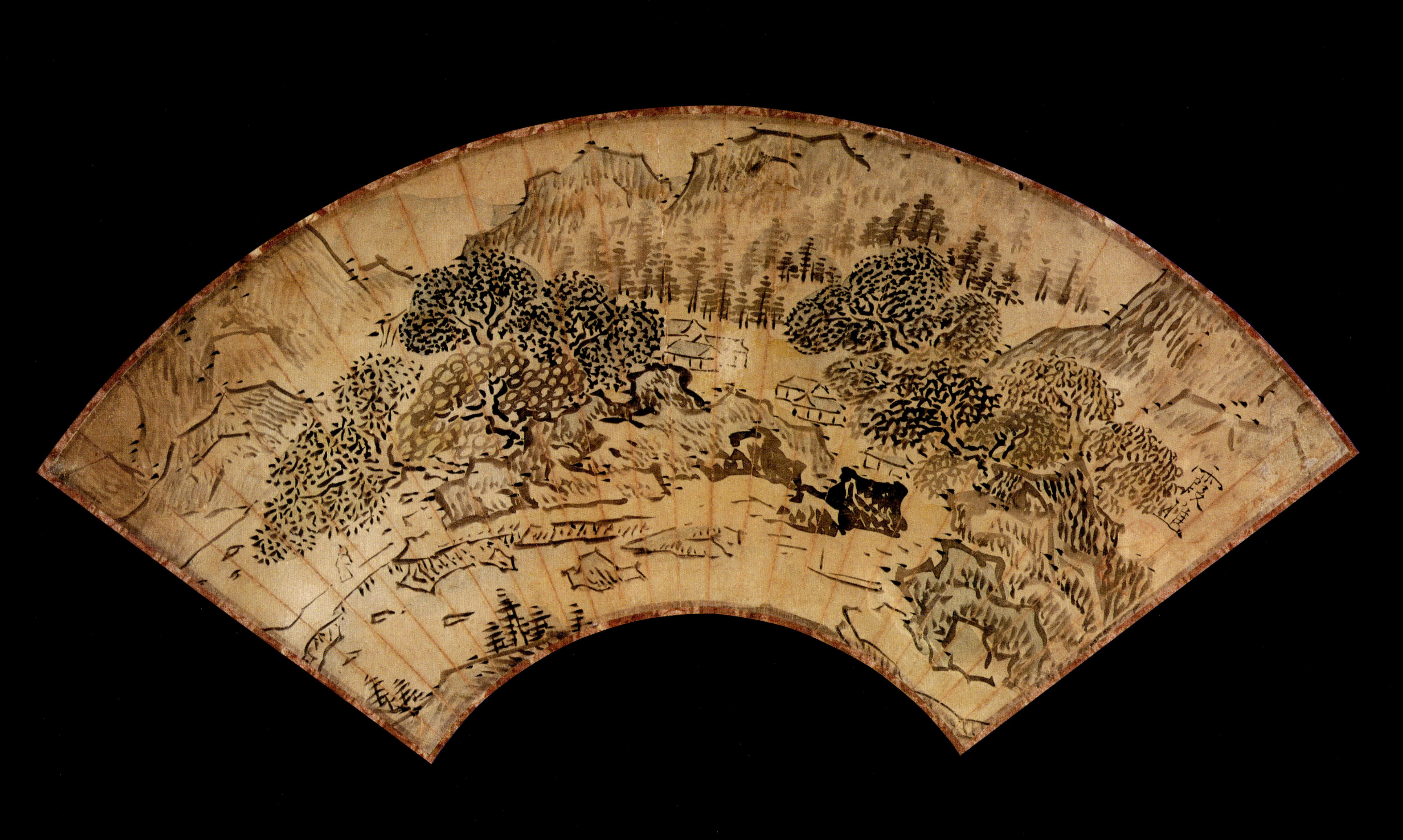

25   Ike Gyokuran, *Landscape*

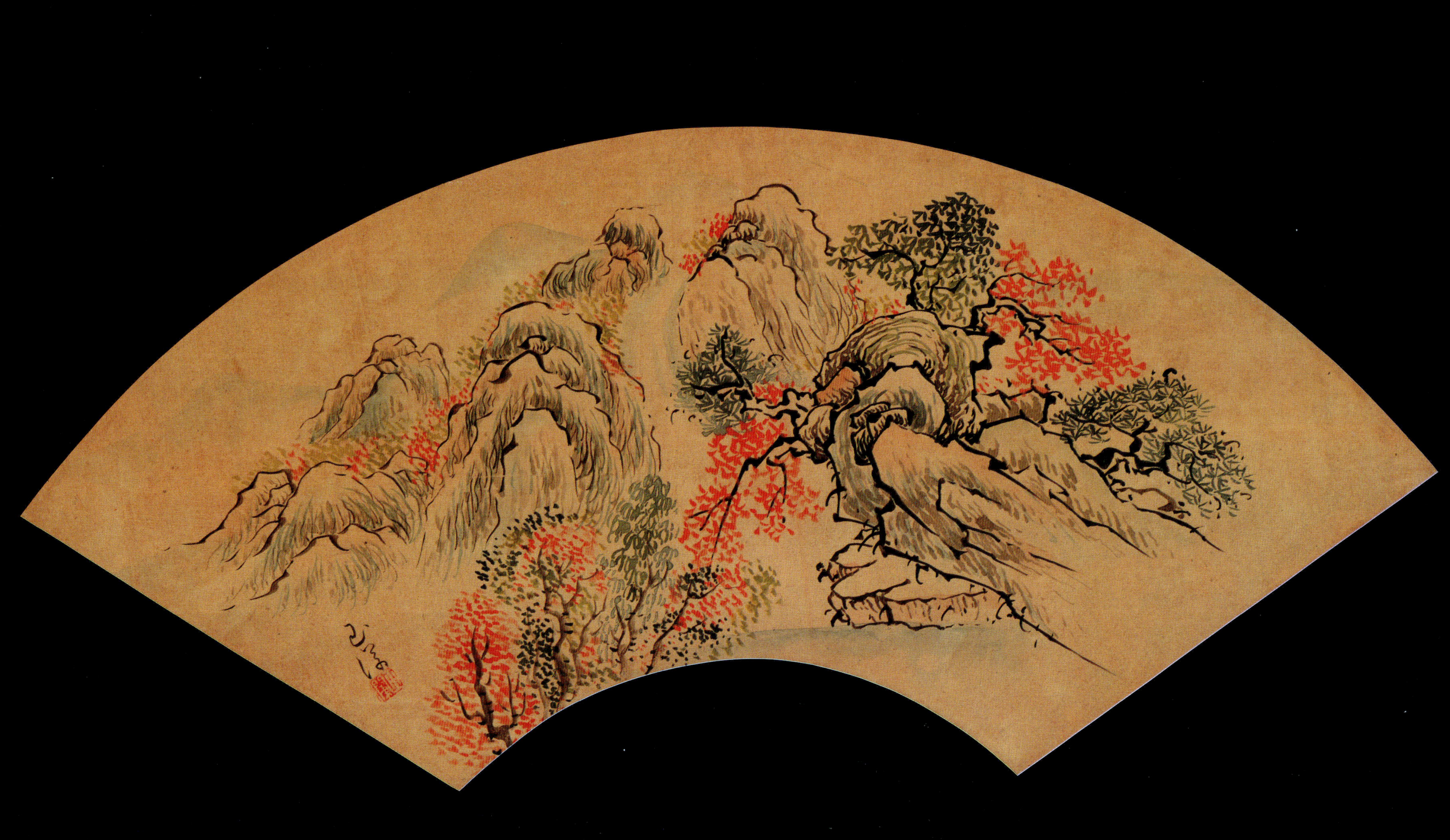

26   Ike Gyokuran, *Akashi Bay*

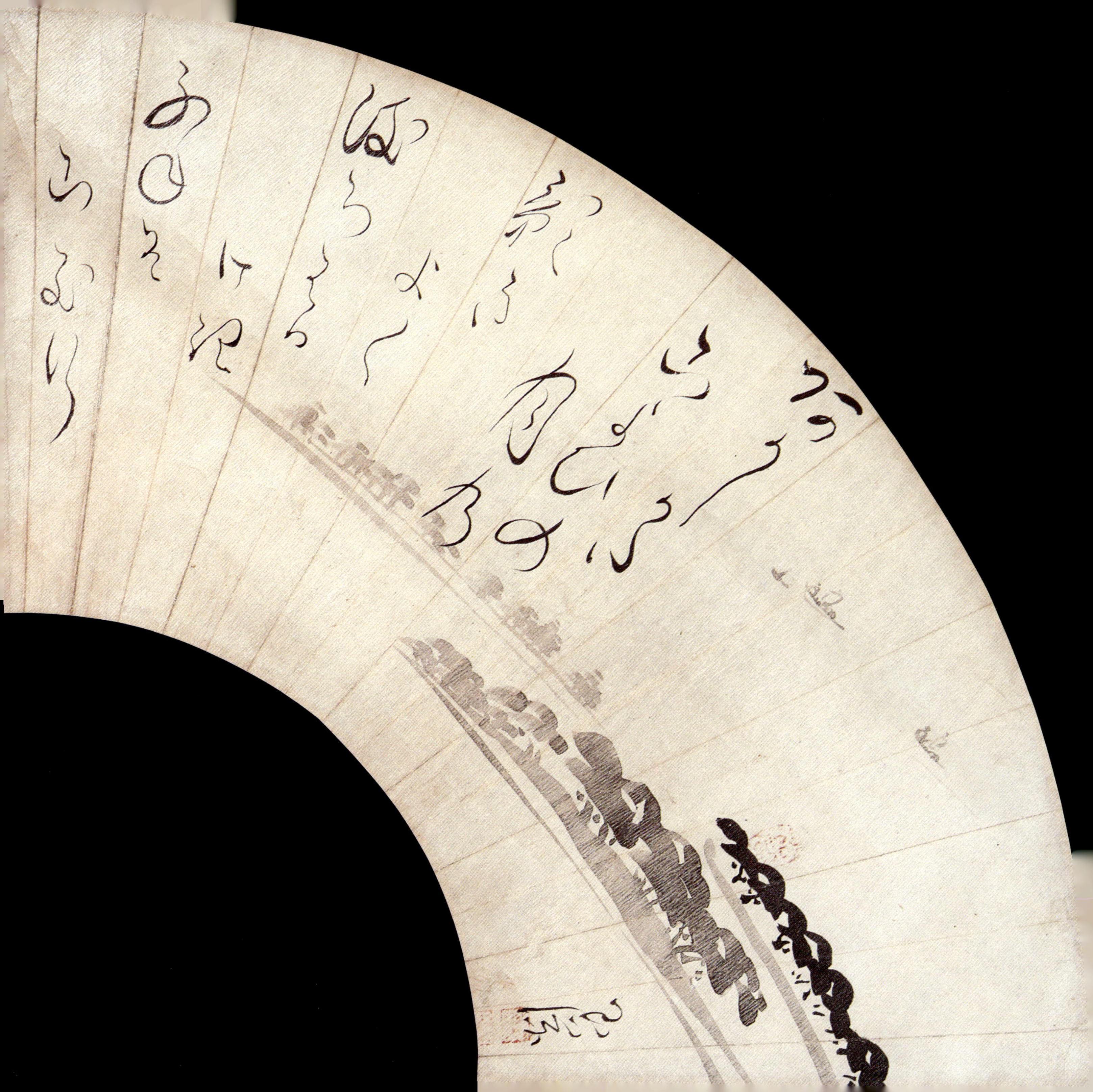

27   Ki Baitei, *Three-Riders in the Rain*

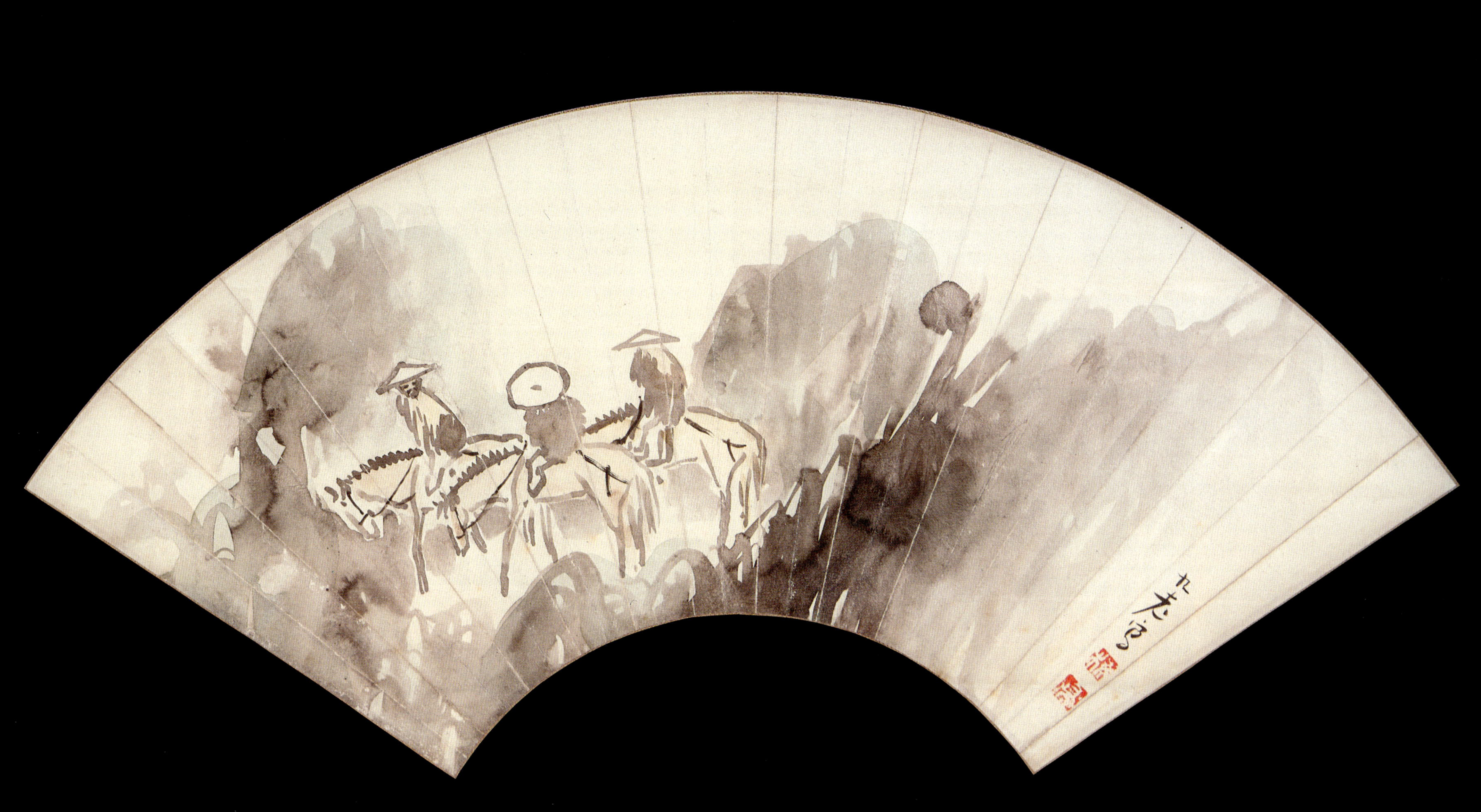

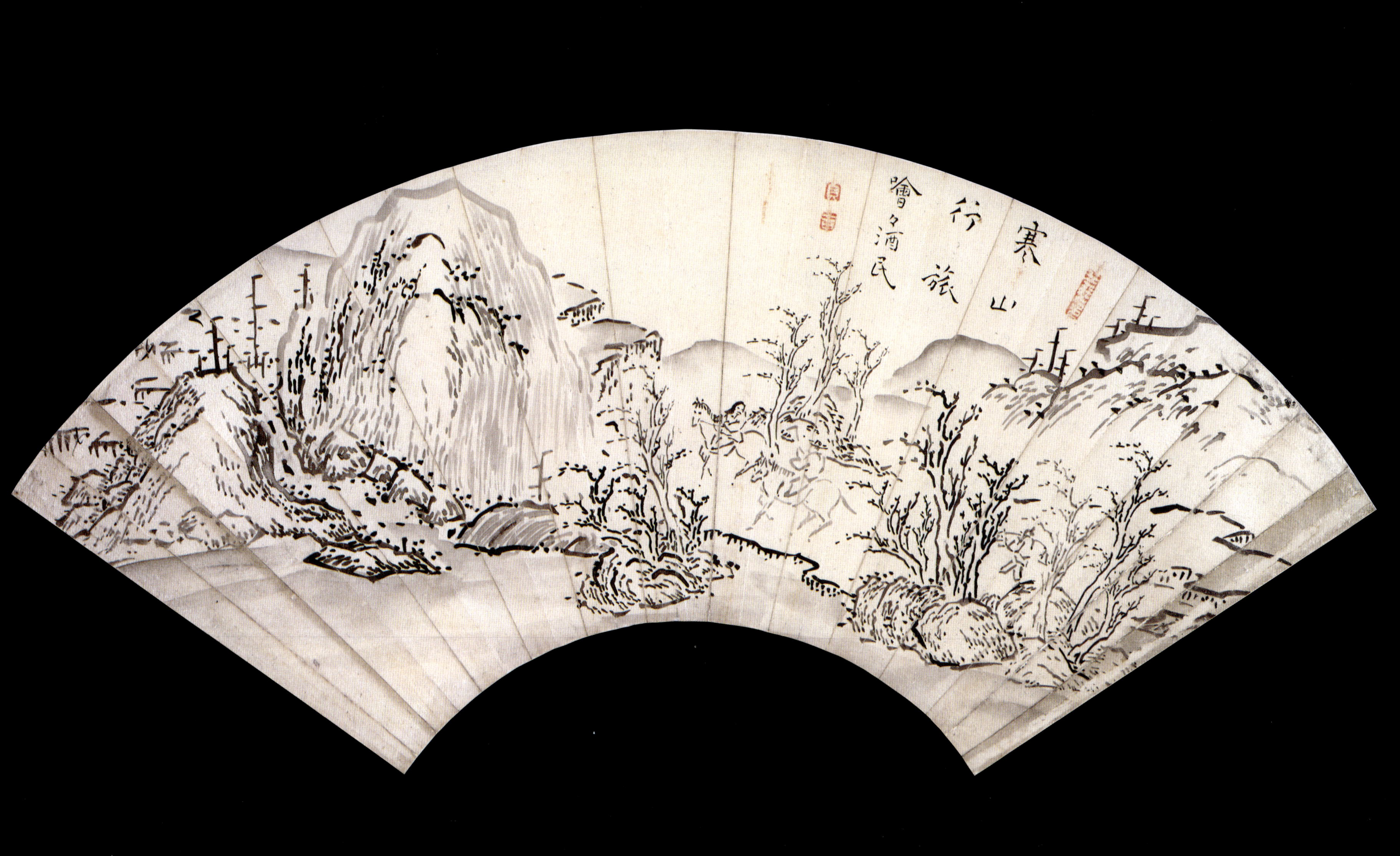
寒山行旅
繪々酒民

29   Okada Beisanjin, *Landscape*

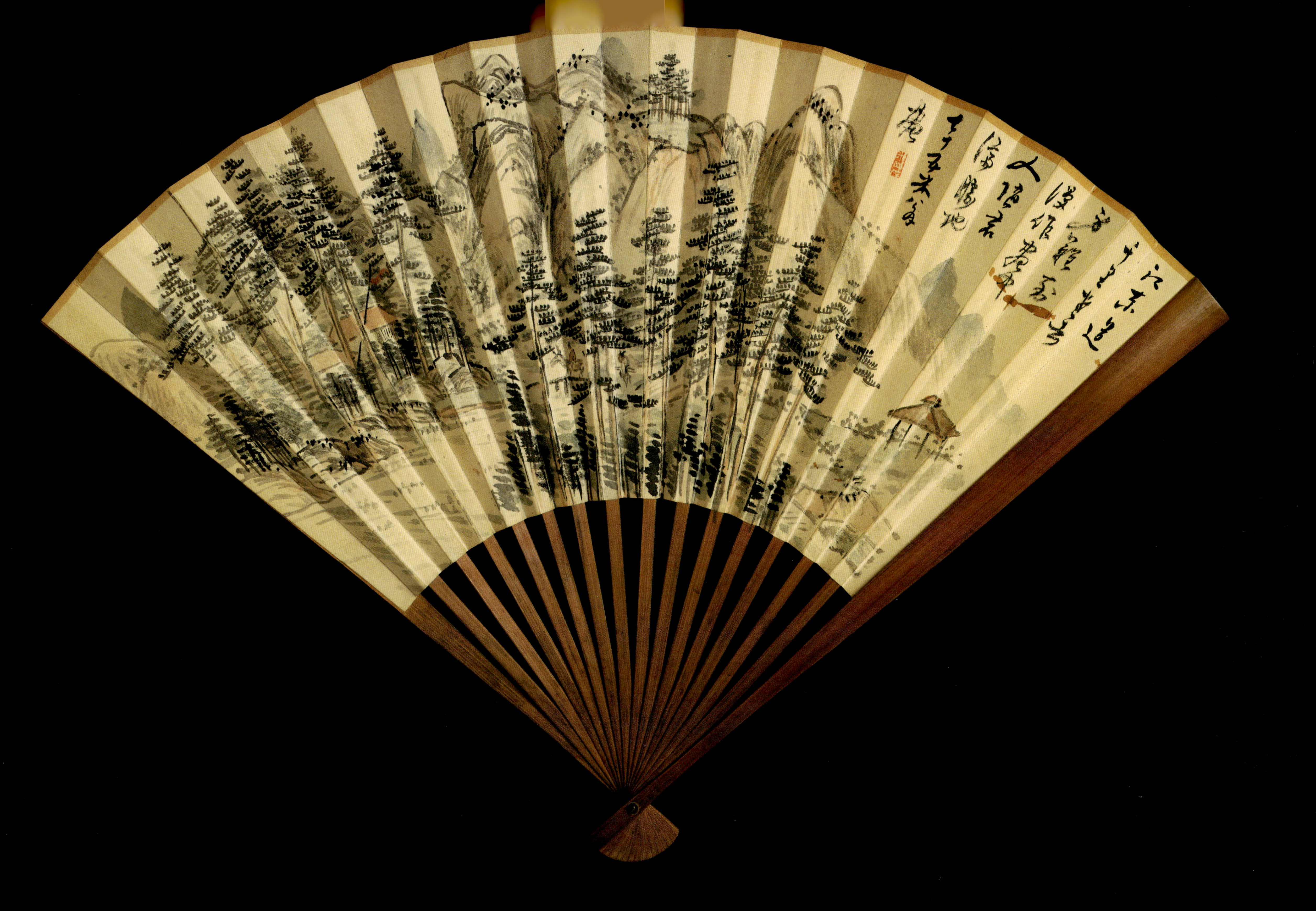

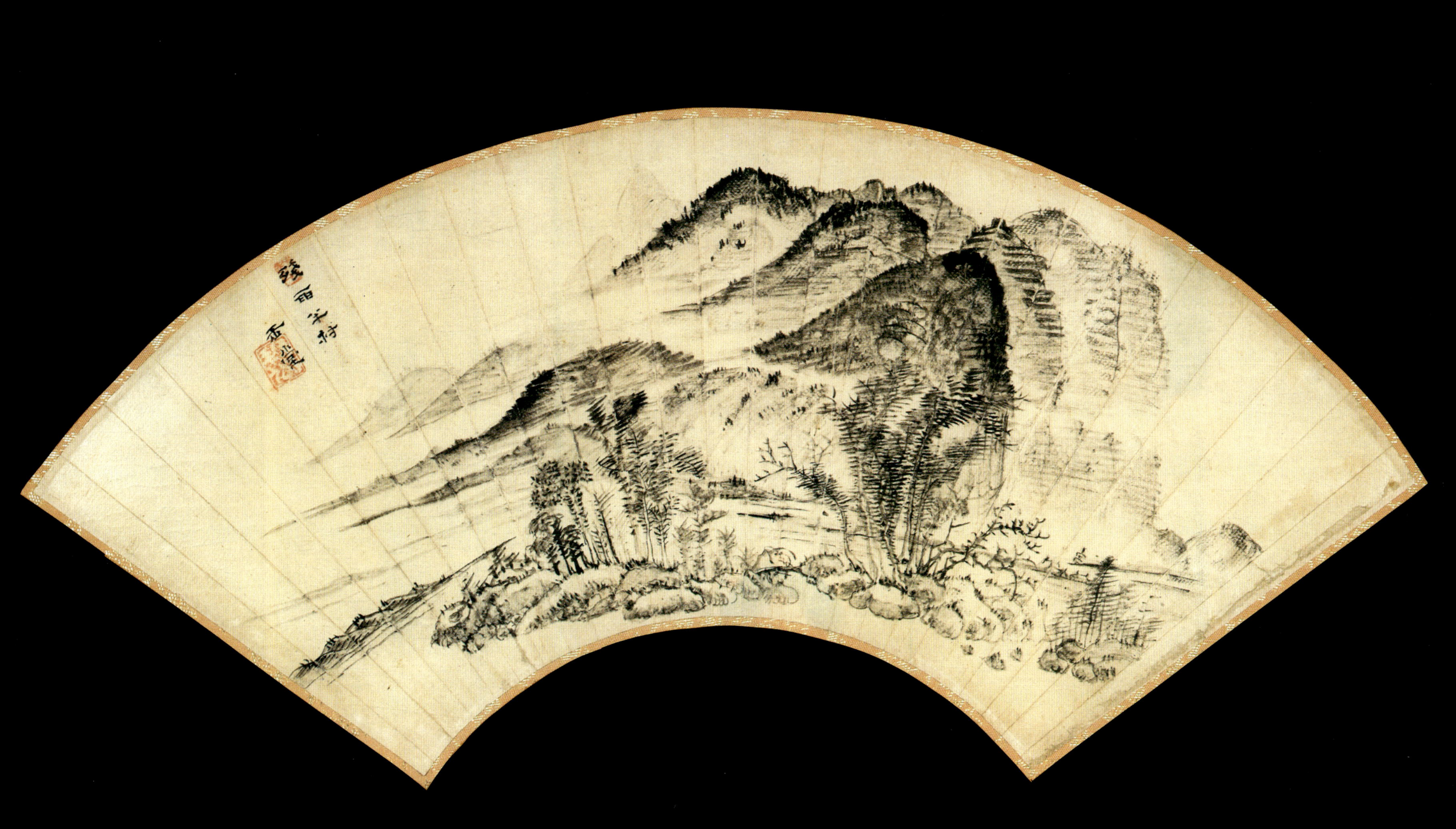

31   Uragami Gyokudō, *Spring Clouds Like Thick Paste*

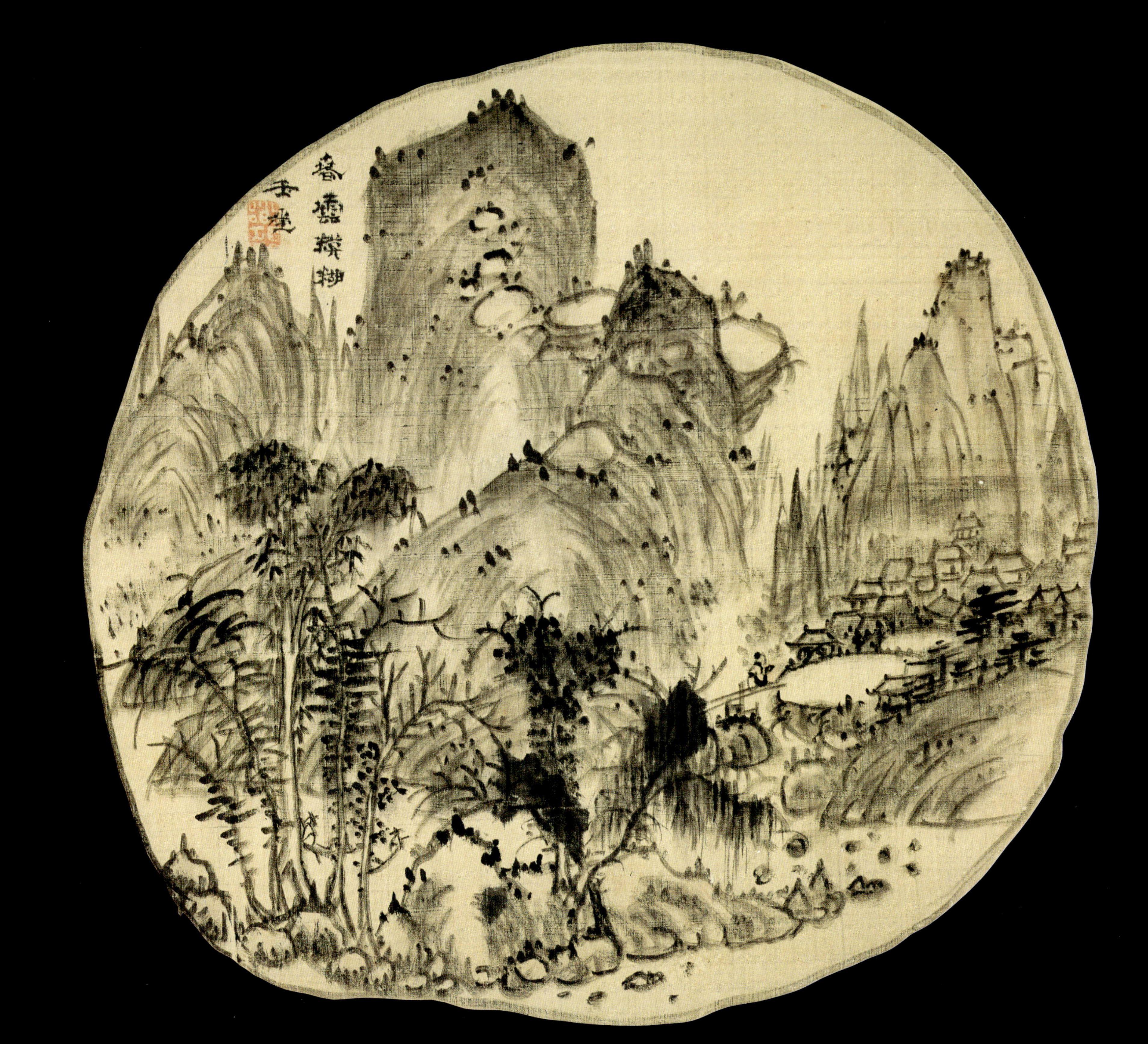

春靄擬柳州
半生

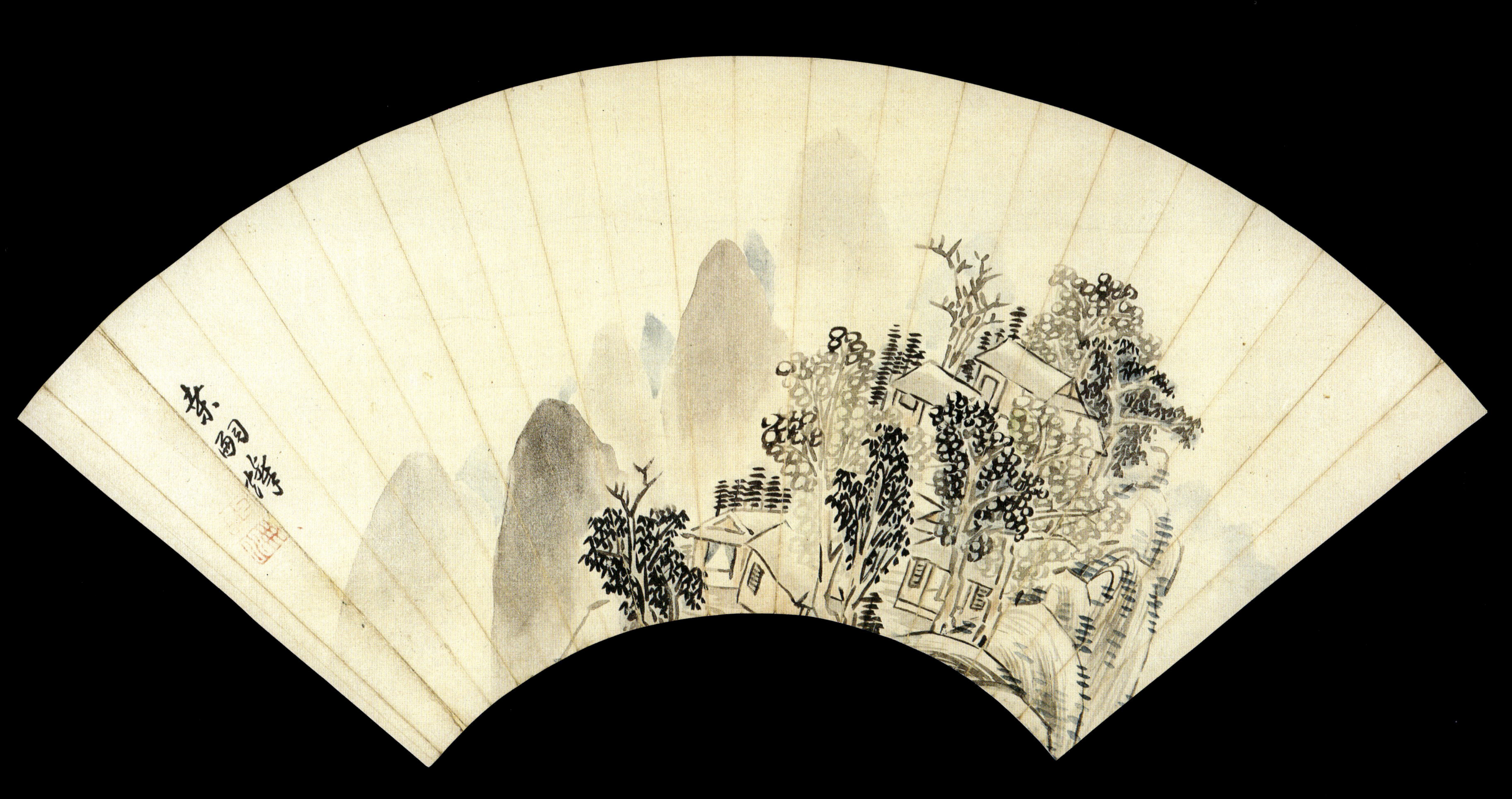

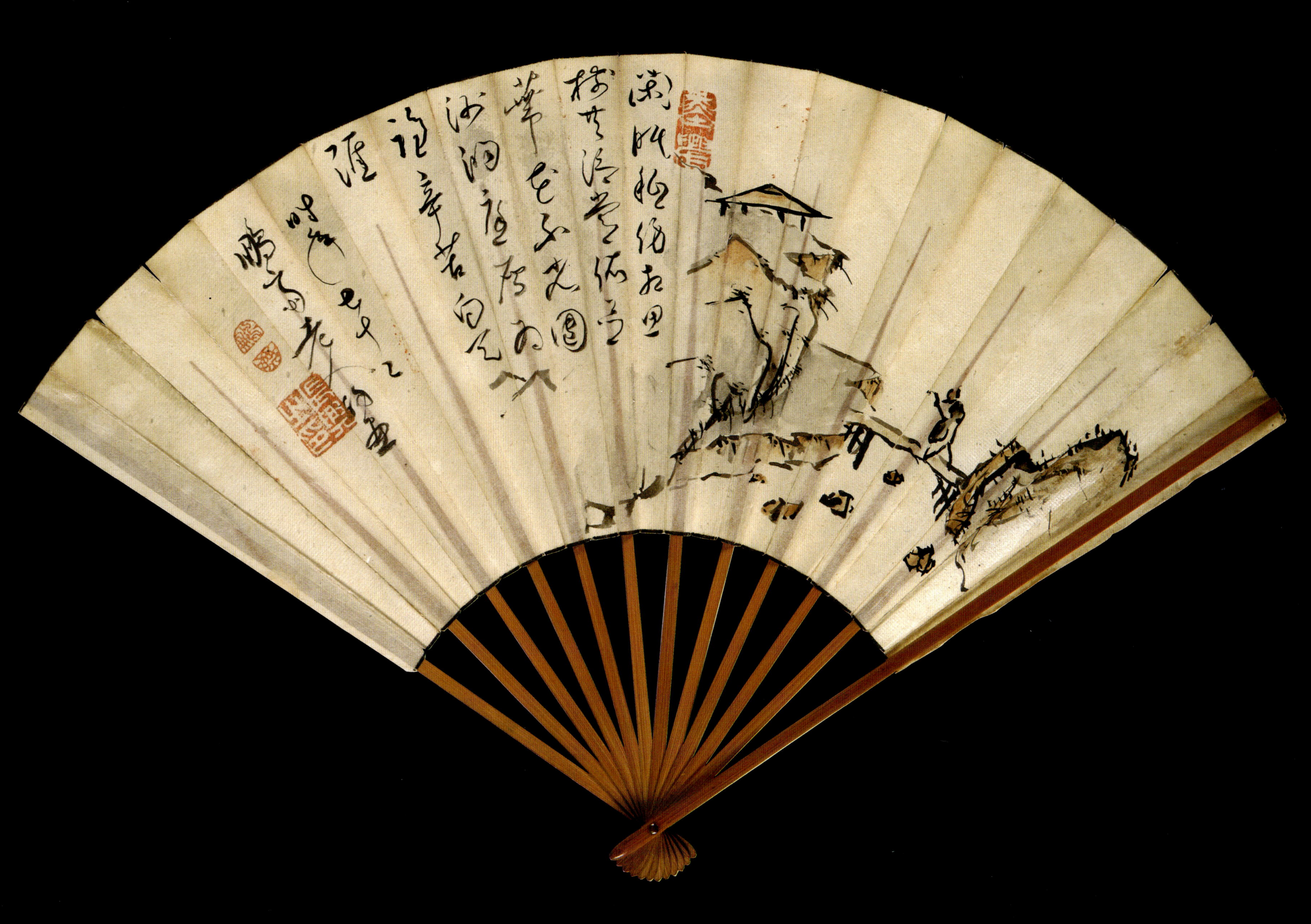

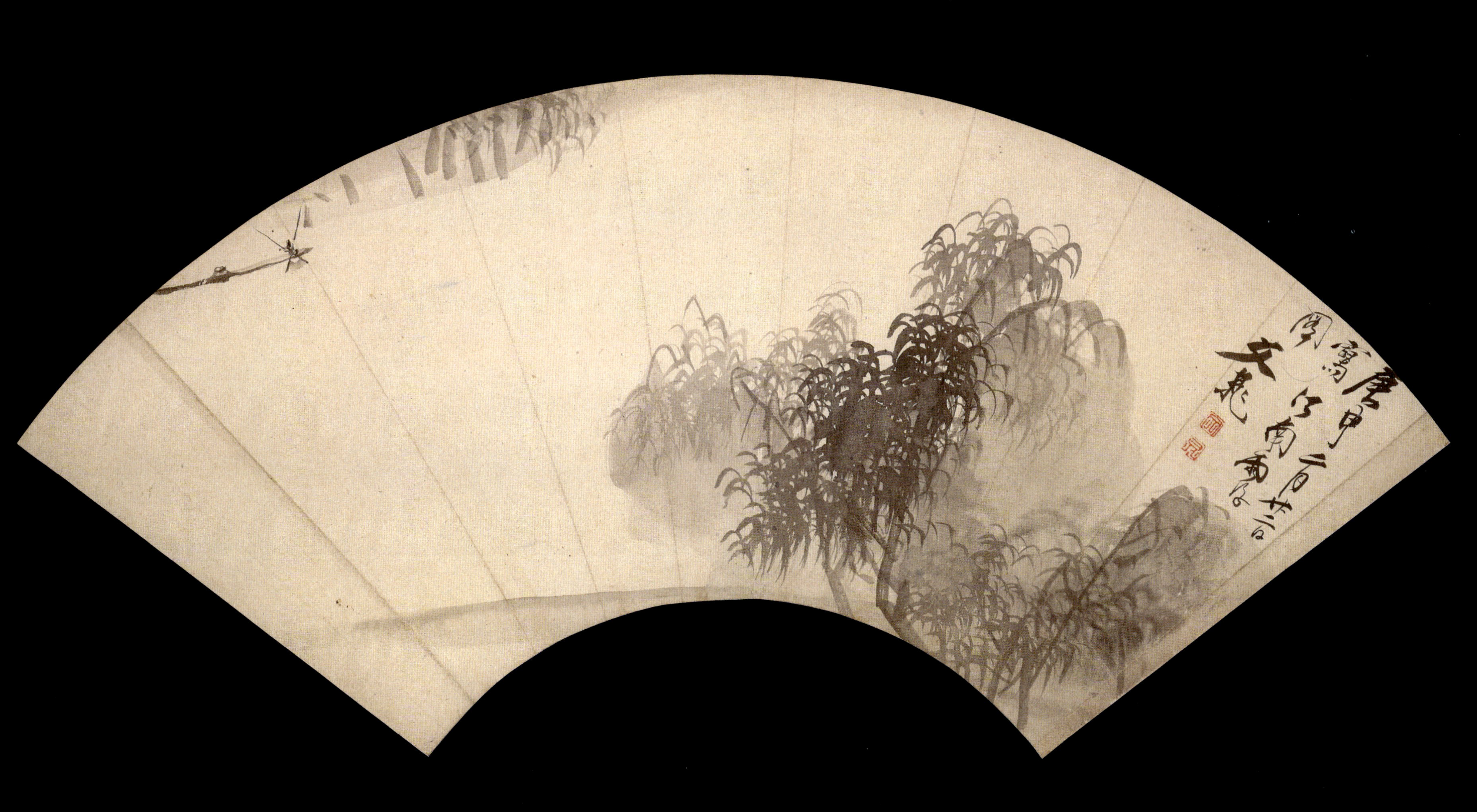

35   Tani Bunchō, *Landscape*

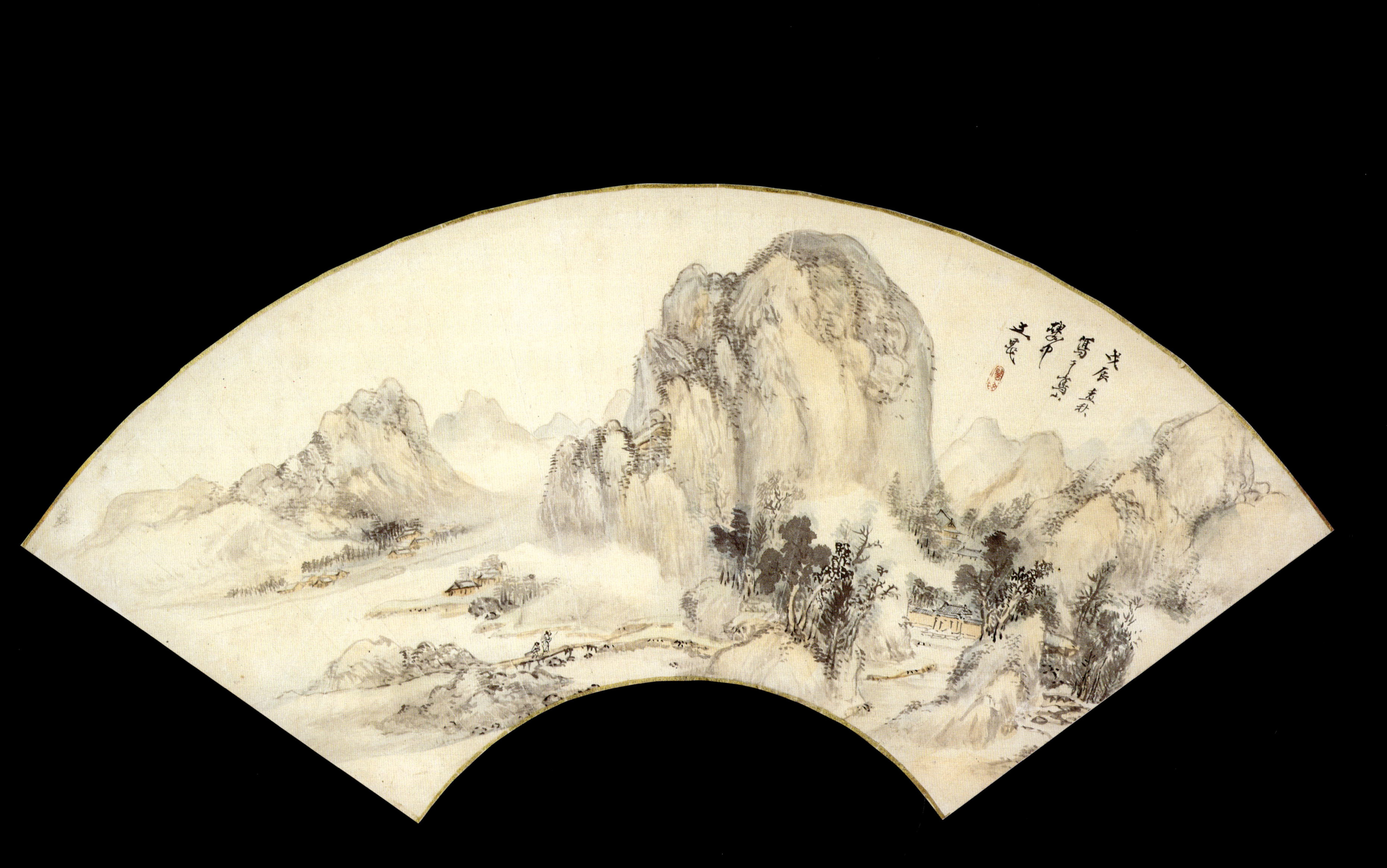

36   Yokoi Kinkoku, *Landscape*

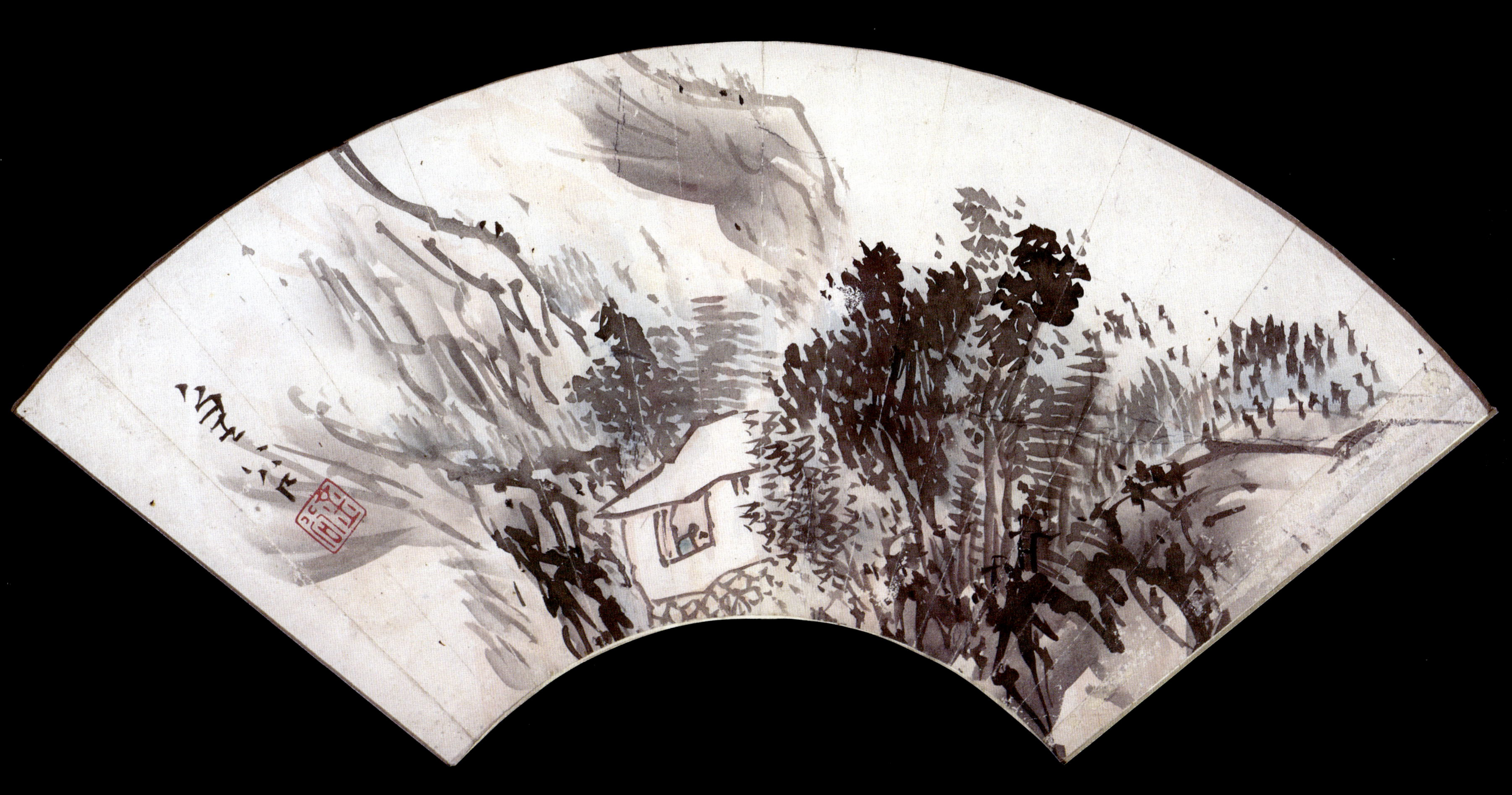

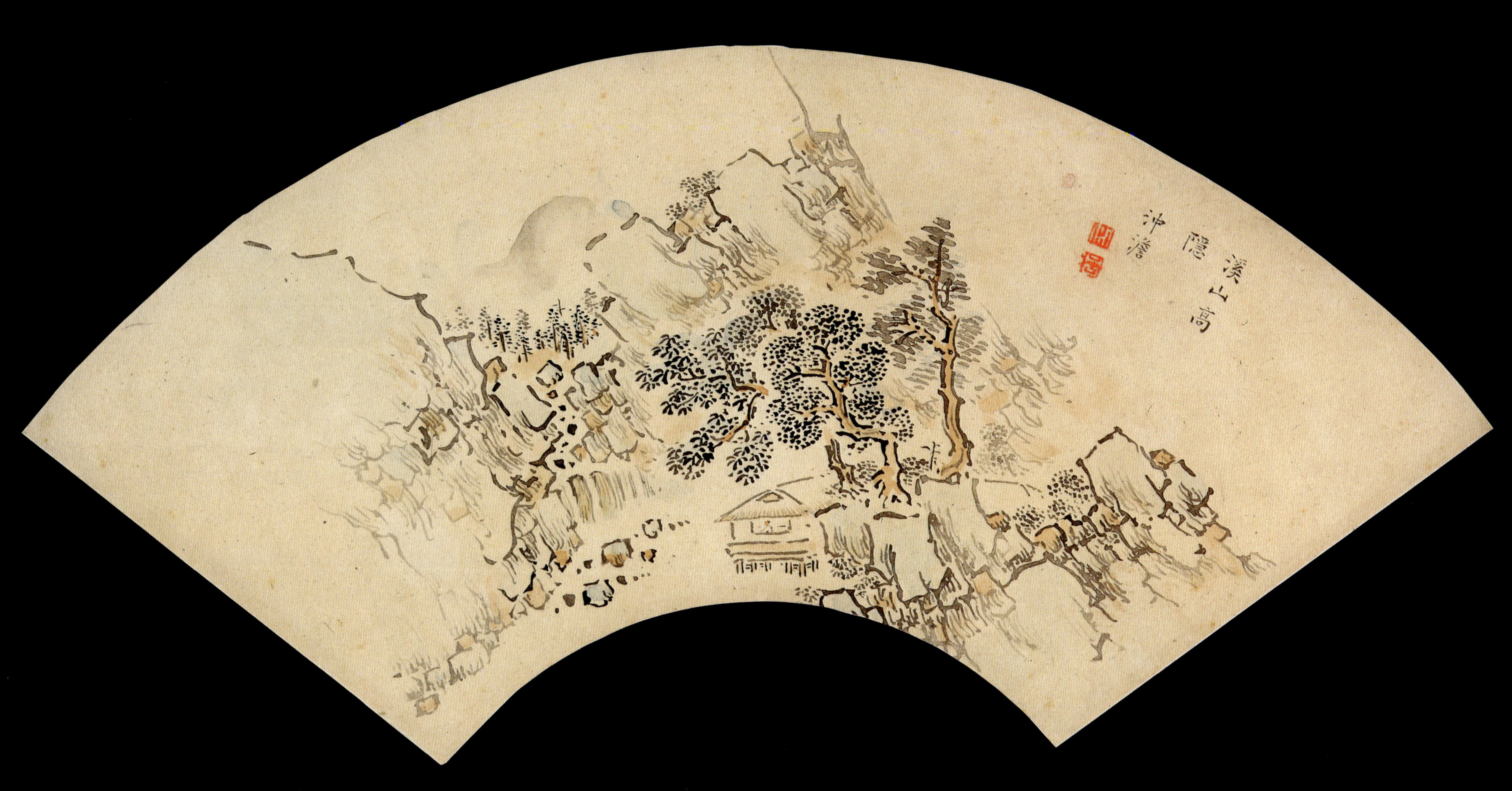
溪上高隱
沖澹寫

38   Nukina Kaioku, *Landscape with Pine Trees*

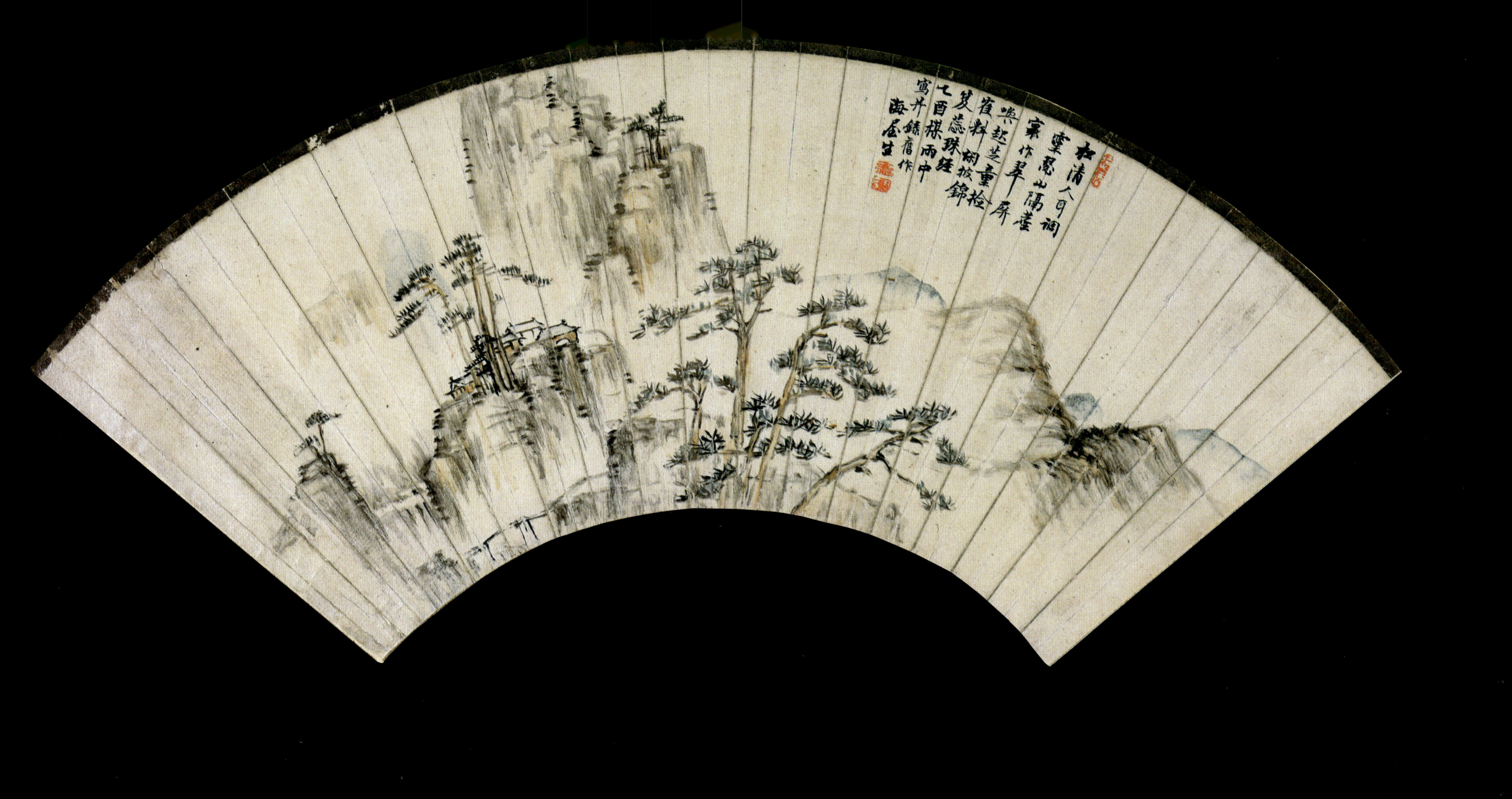

松涛人可調
寒作翠一屏
靈感山隔基
歎料網披錦
雀蕊珠經
七酉棋雨中
寫升録庵作
海屋生

39   Okada Hankō, *Landscape*

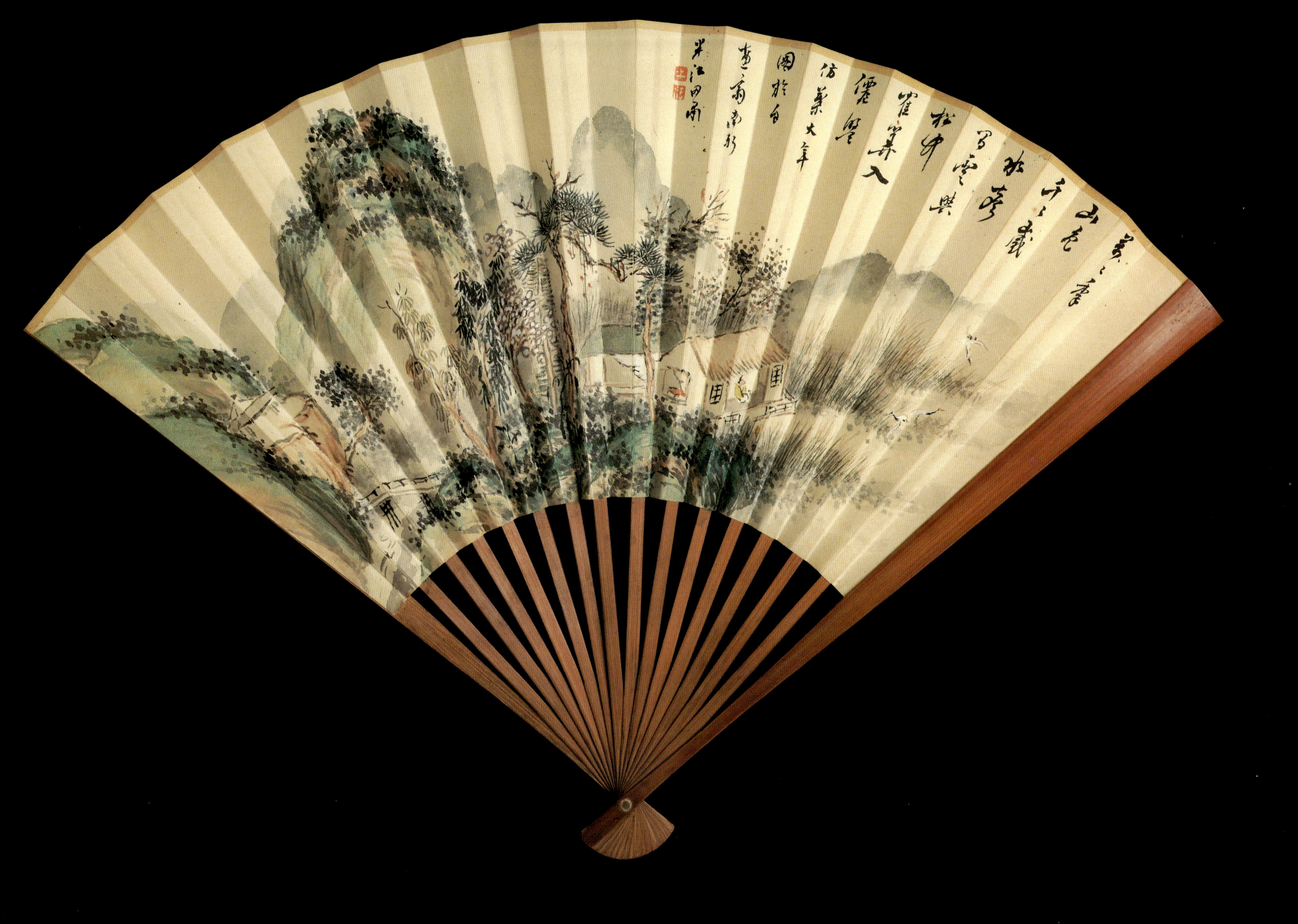

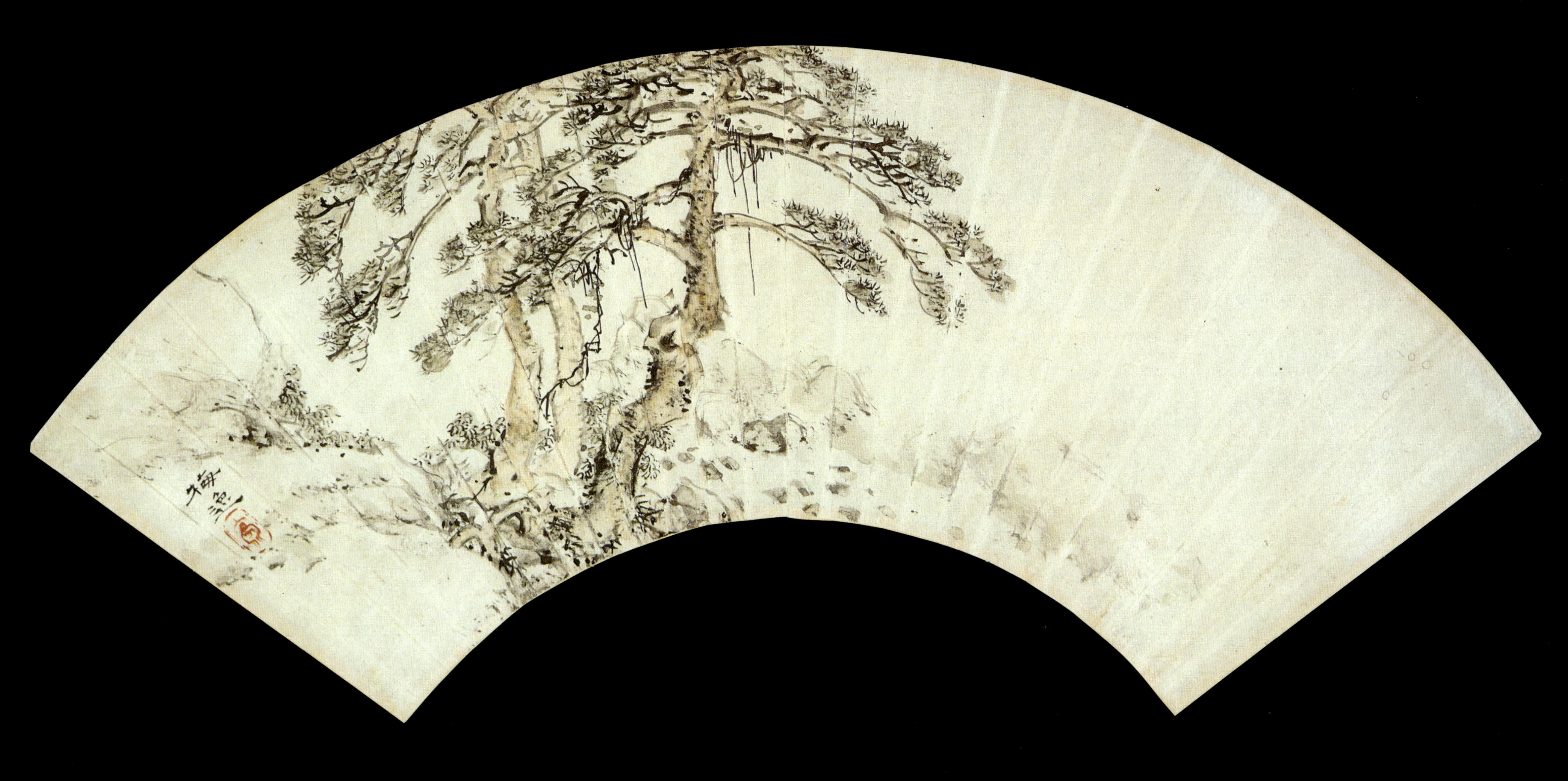

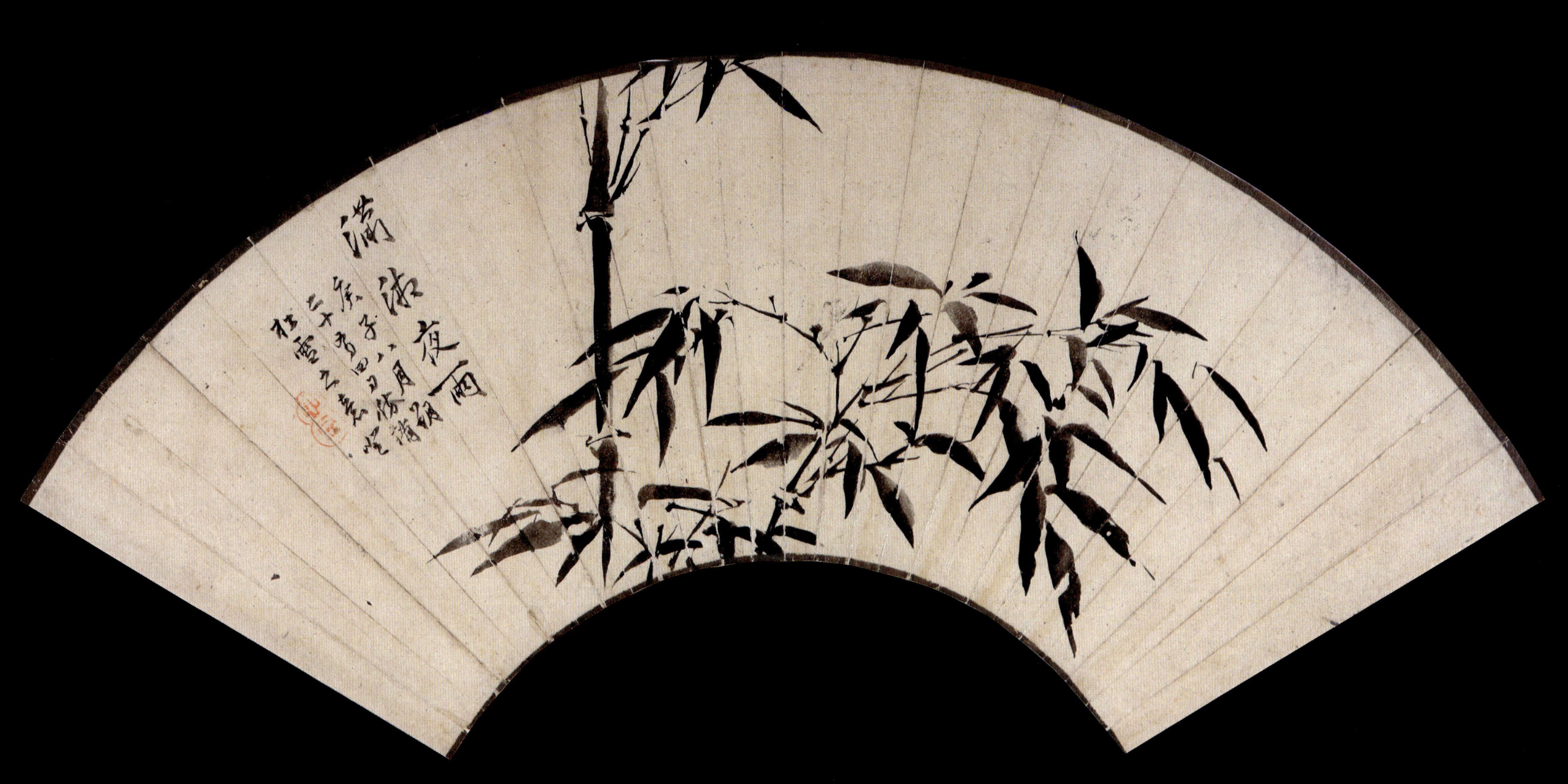

瀟瀟夜雨
癸子八月
三十九日防滿
松庵作畫
逞滿頌

42   Watanabe Kazan, *Portrait of Kō Sūkoku*

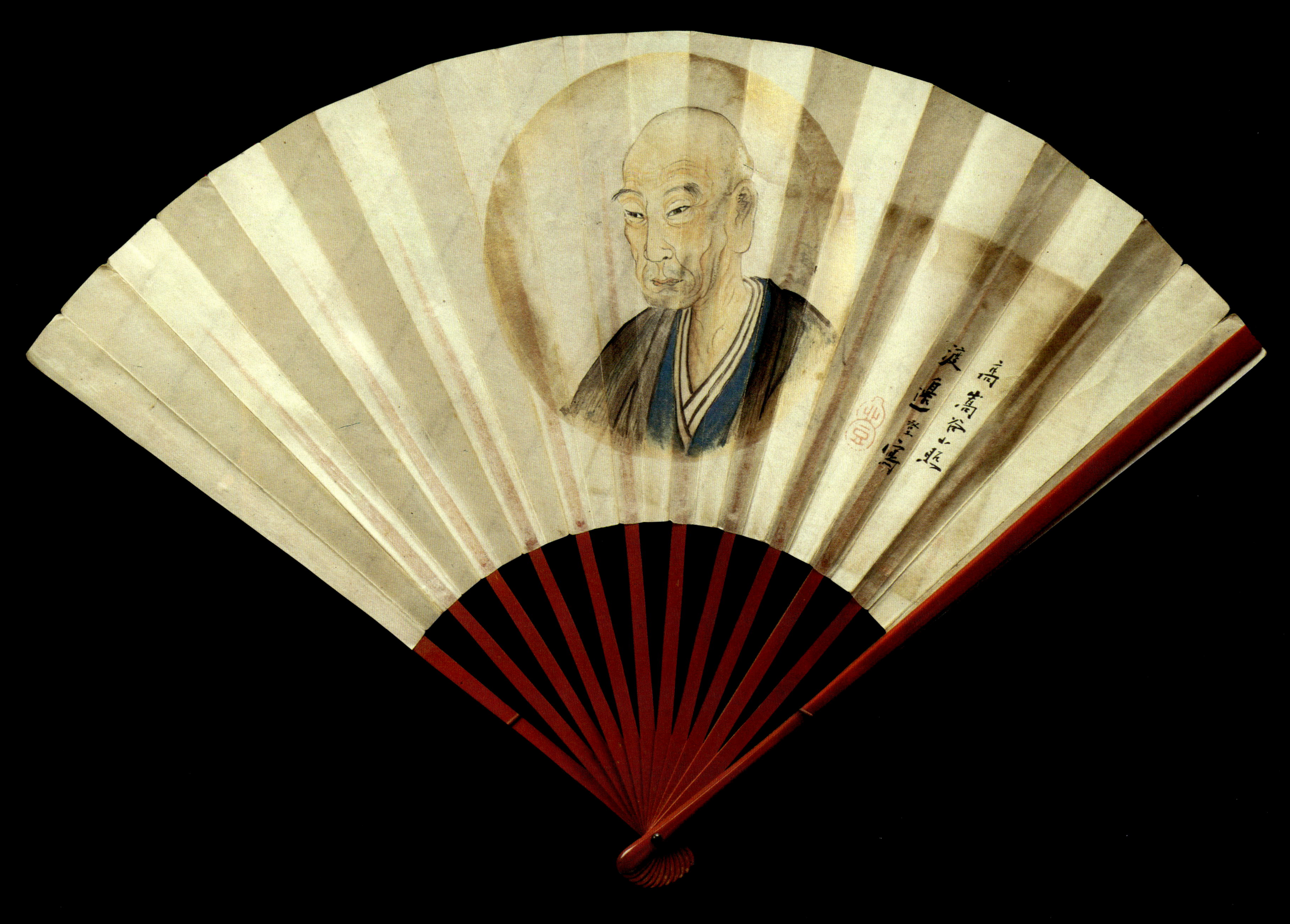

43   Haruki Nanmei, *Landscape*

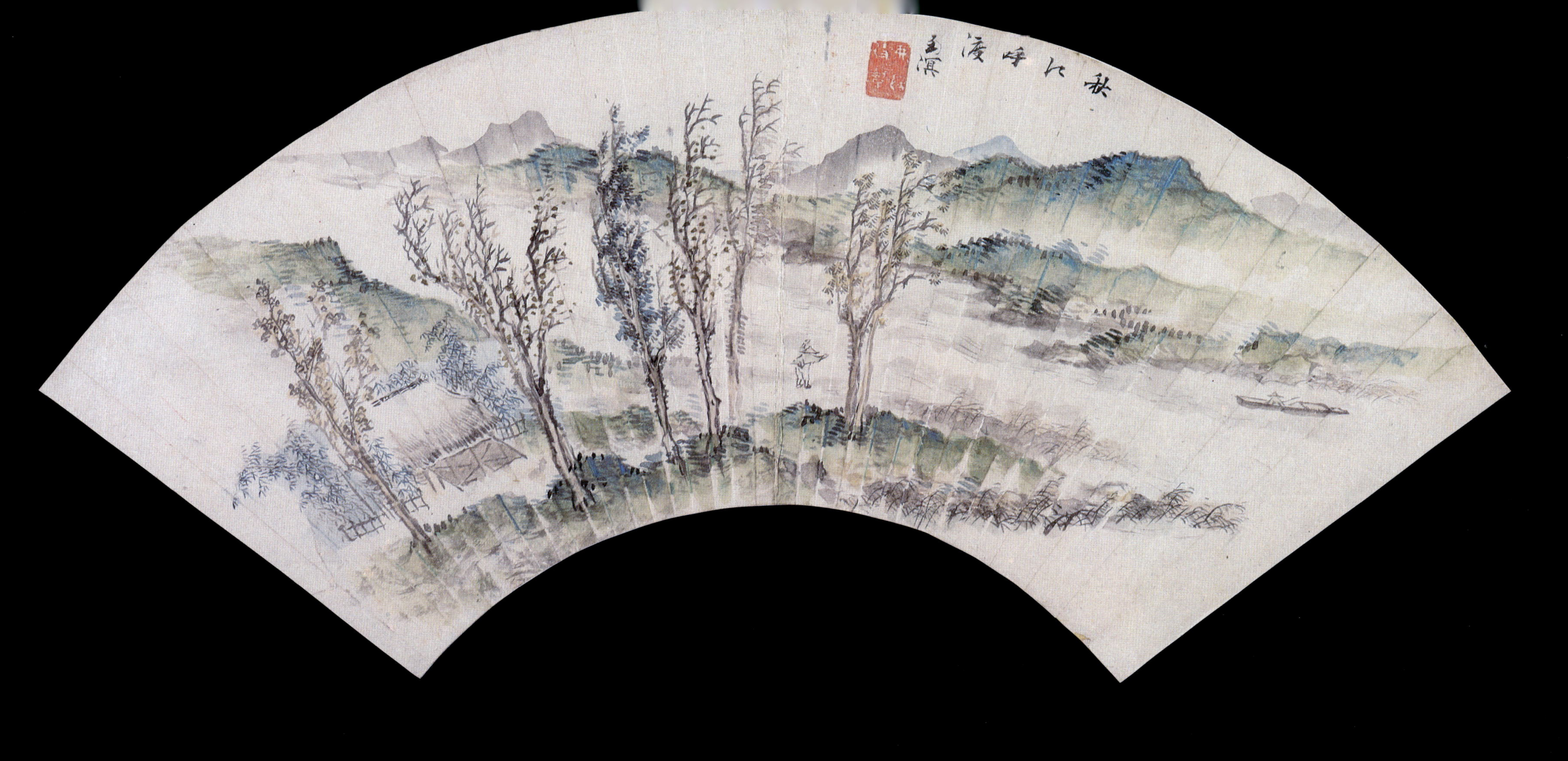
秋山凌峰
王溪

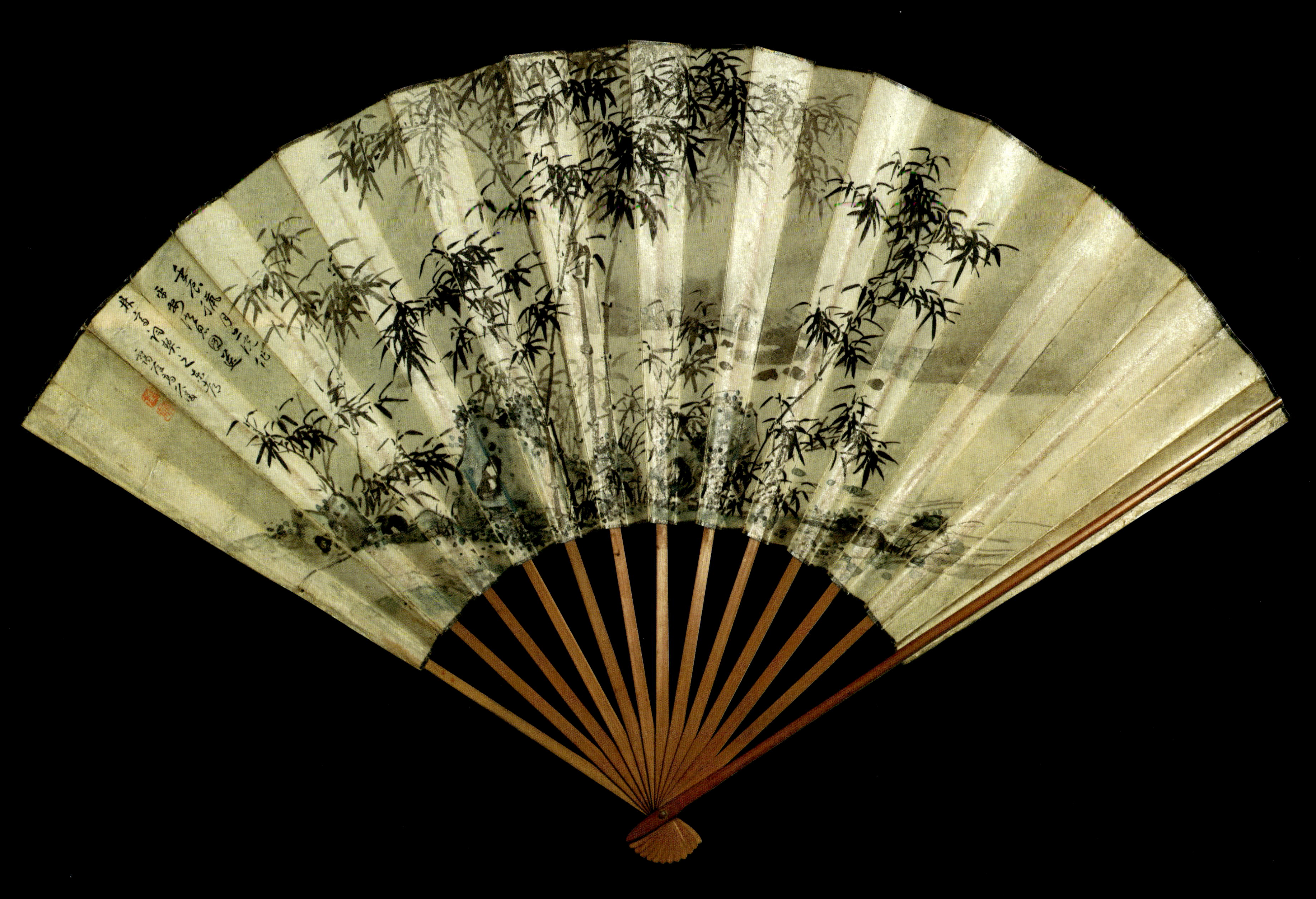

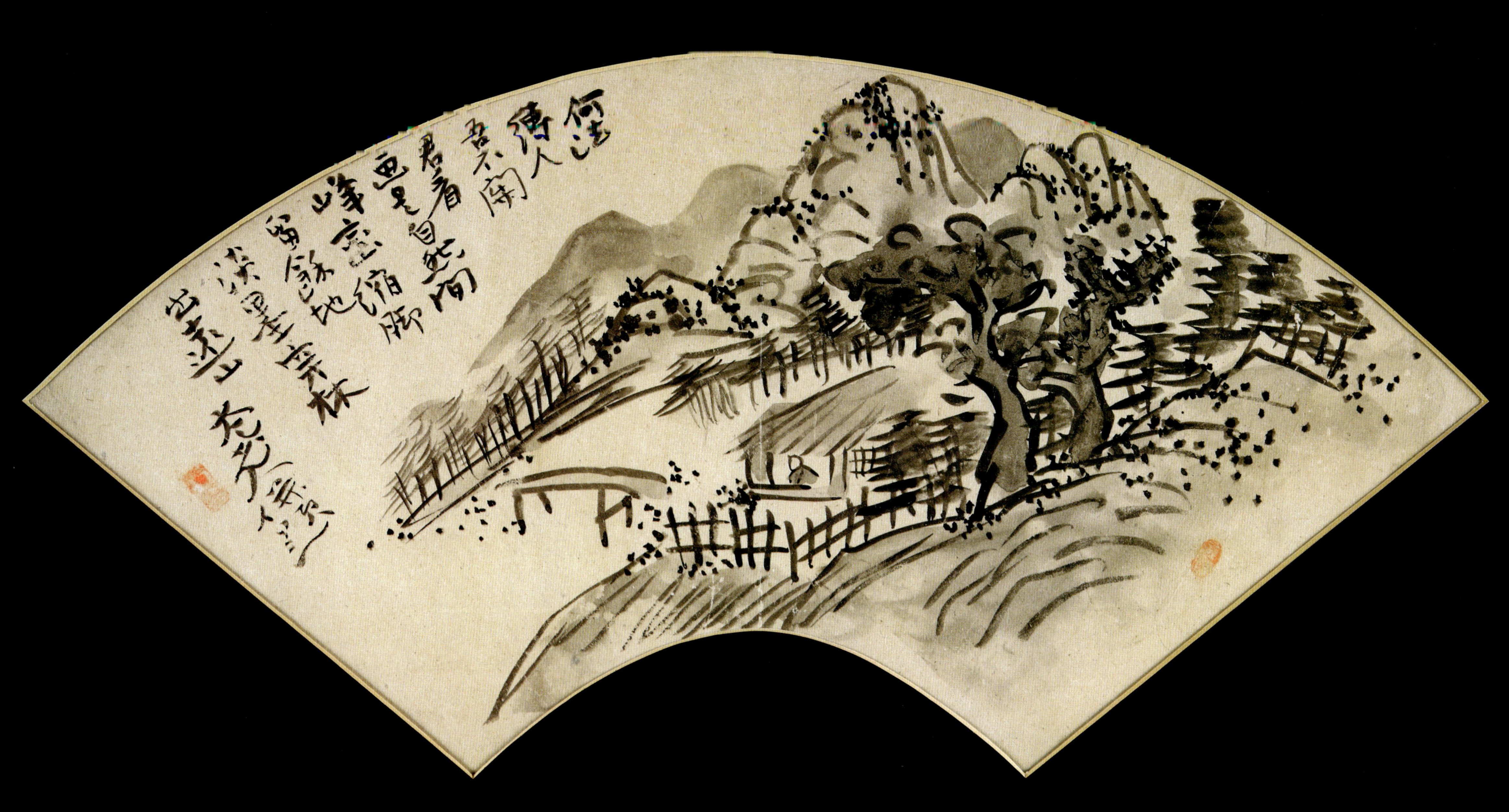

MARUYAMA-SHIJŌ

46   Nagasawa Rosetsu, *Dragon Emerging from Clouds*

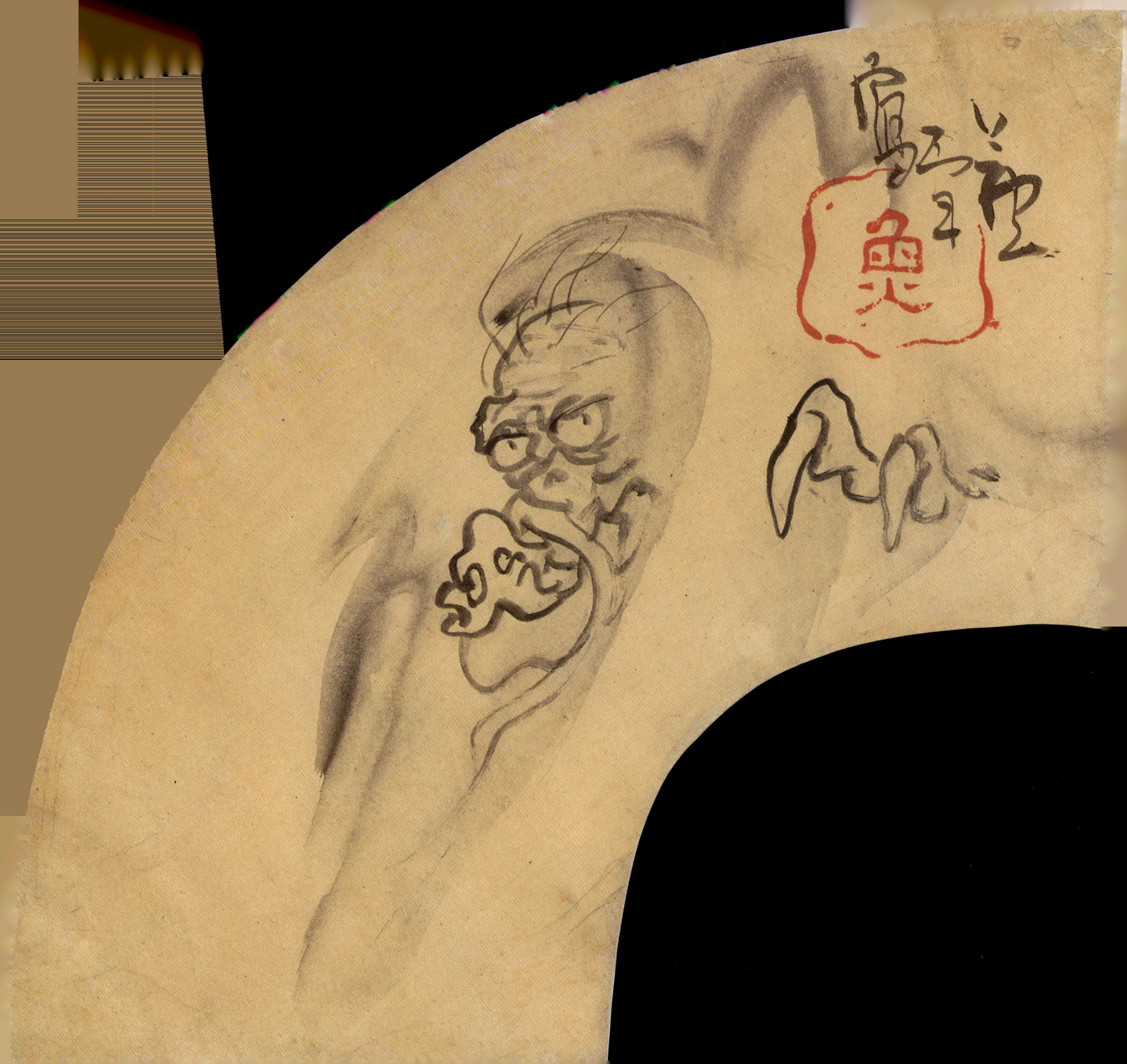

47   Nagasawa Rosetsu, *Landscape*

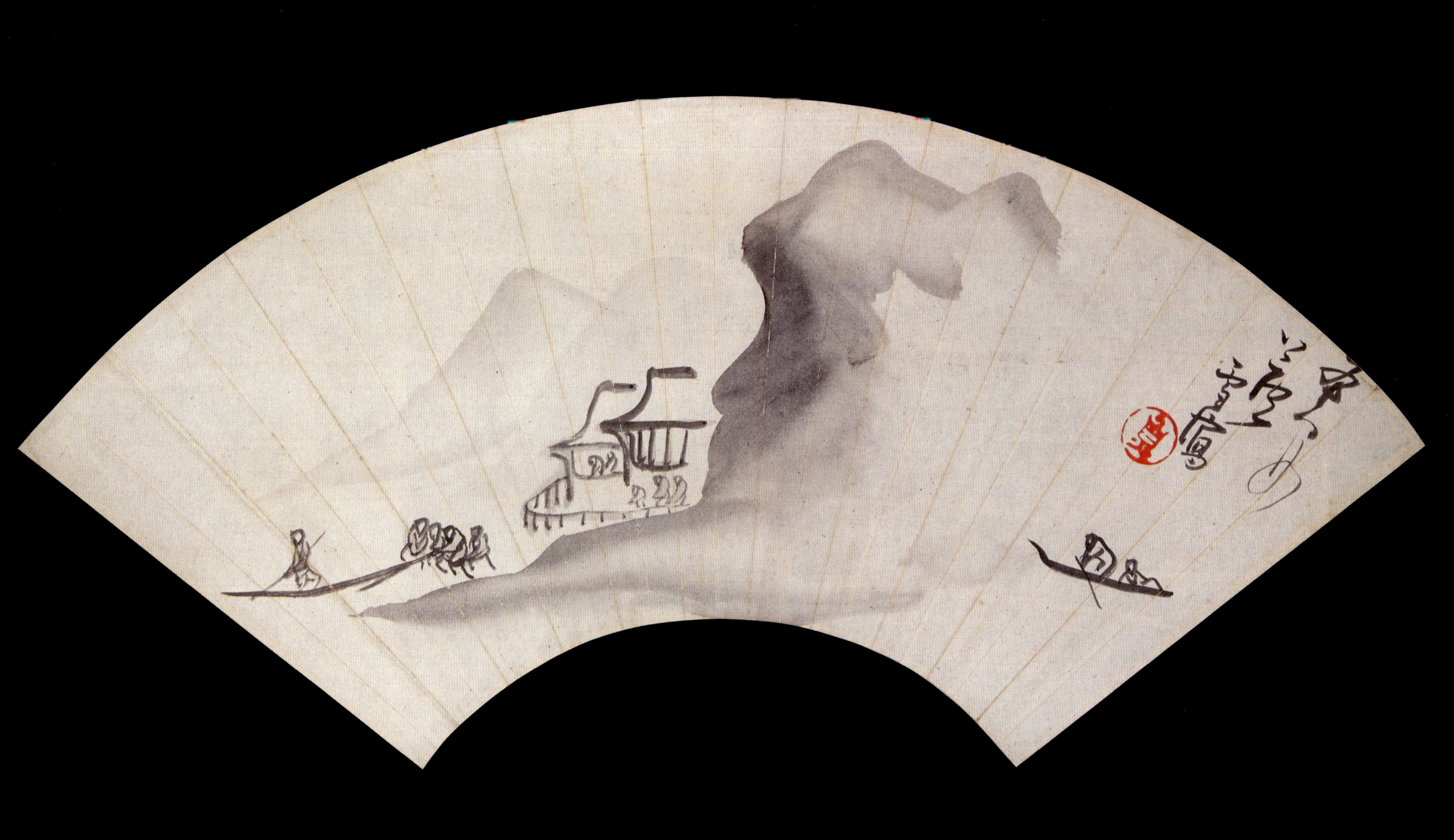

48   Watanabe Nangaku, *Courtesan in Boat*

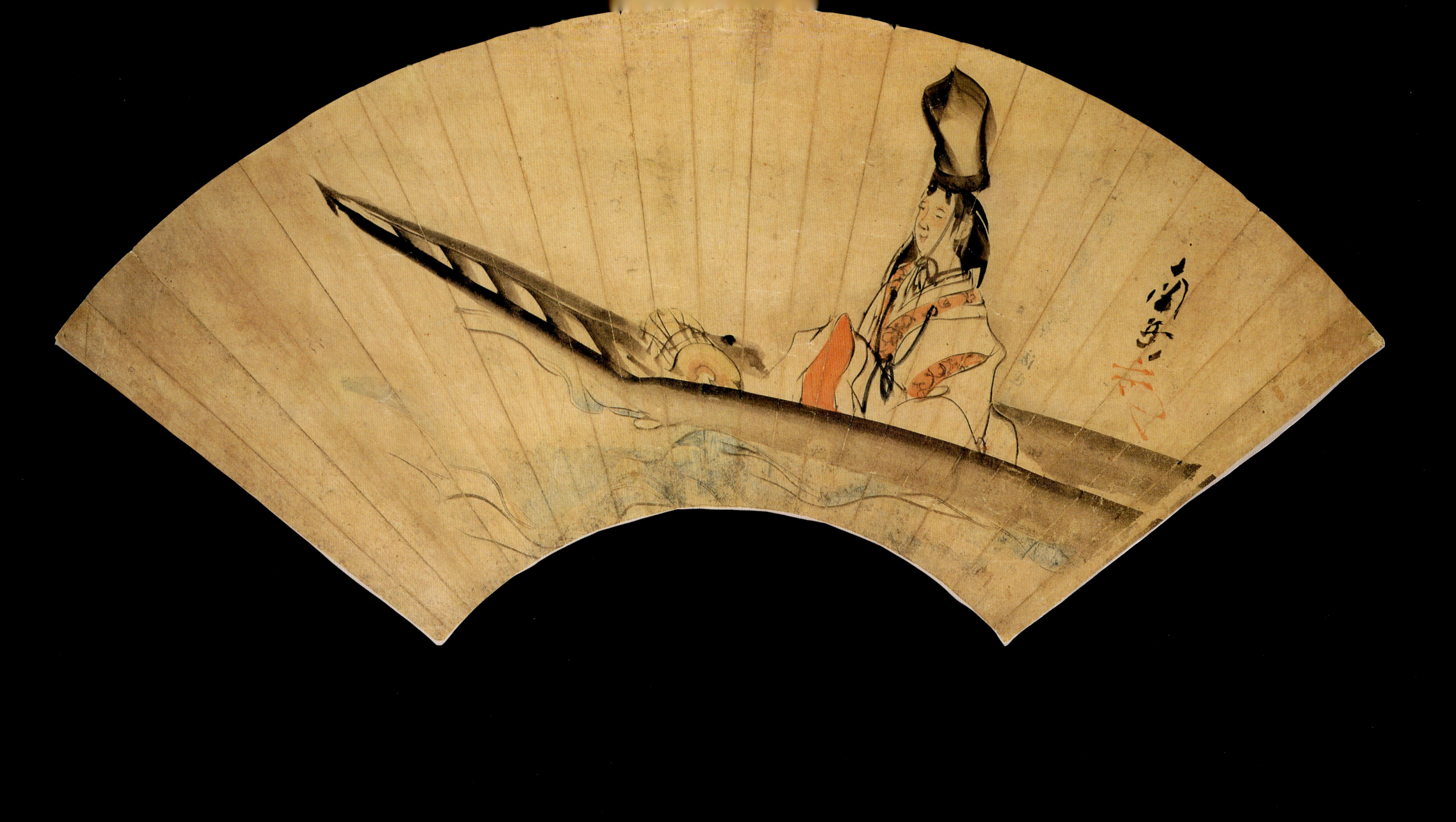

49   Shibata Gitō, *Two Dancers*

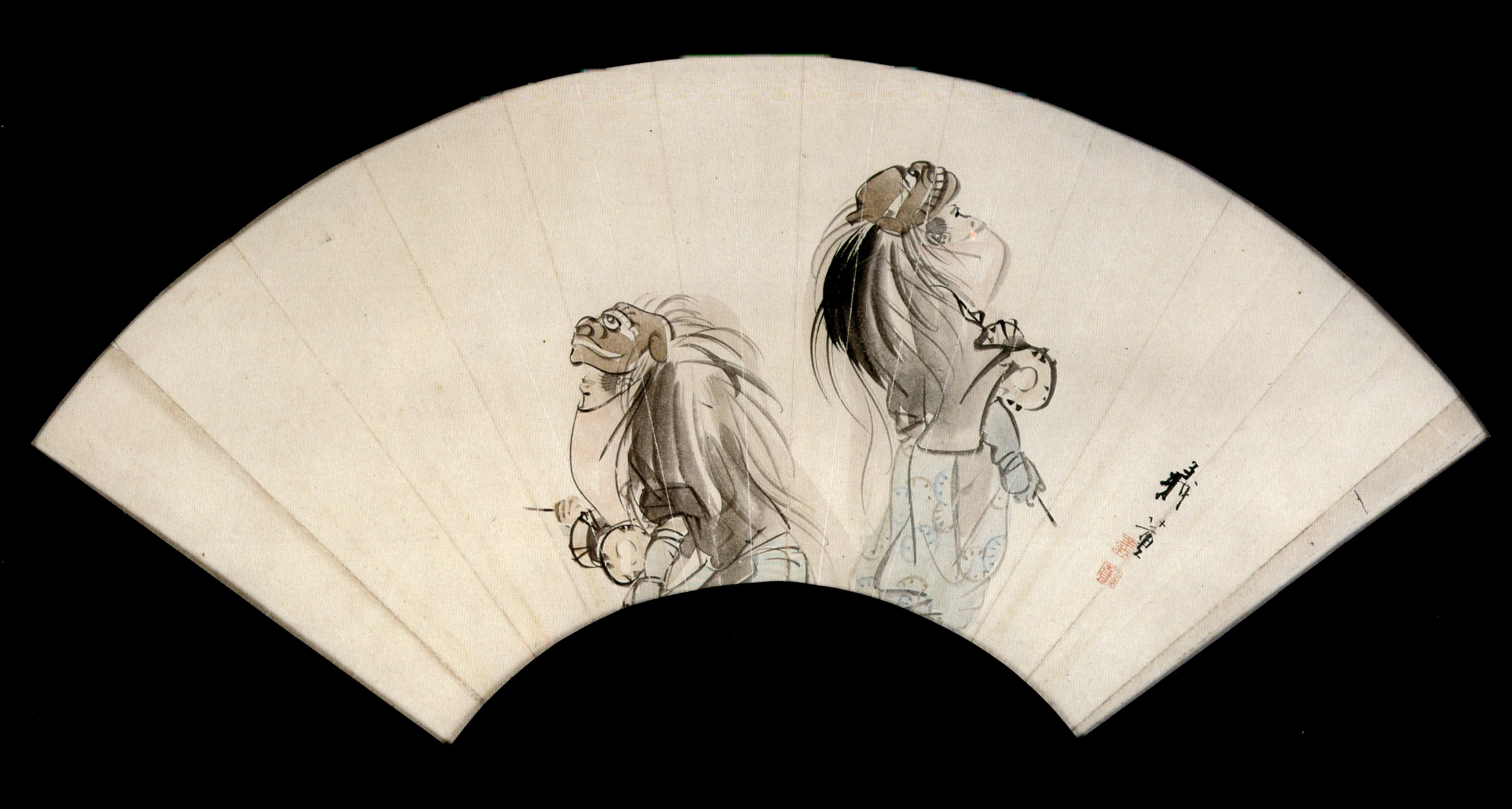

50   Ōnishi Chinnen, *Mount Fuji*

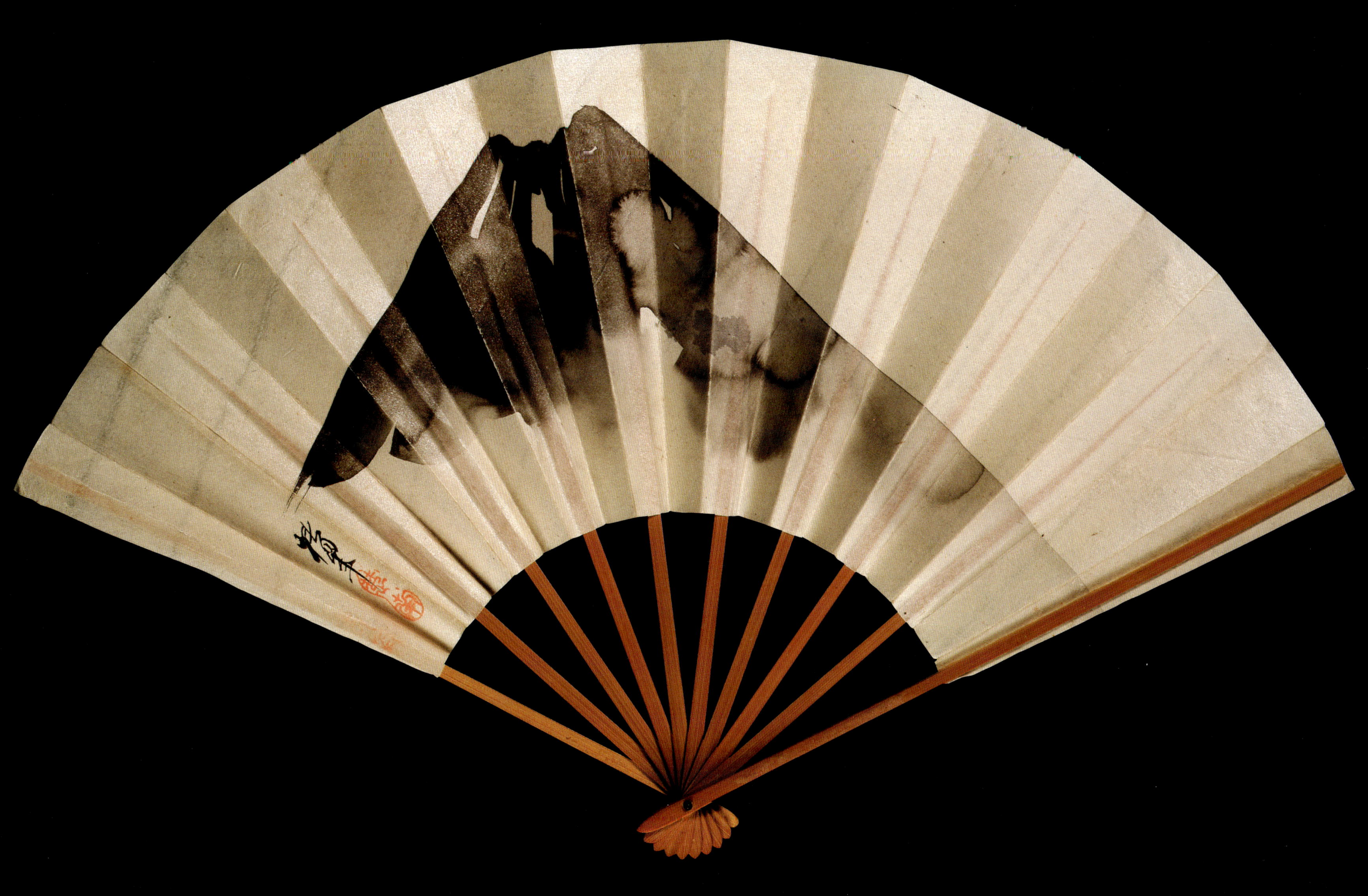

51   Kishi Renzan, *Boatmen in a Winter Landscape*

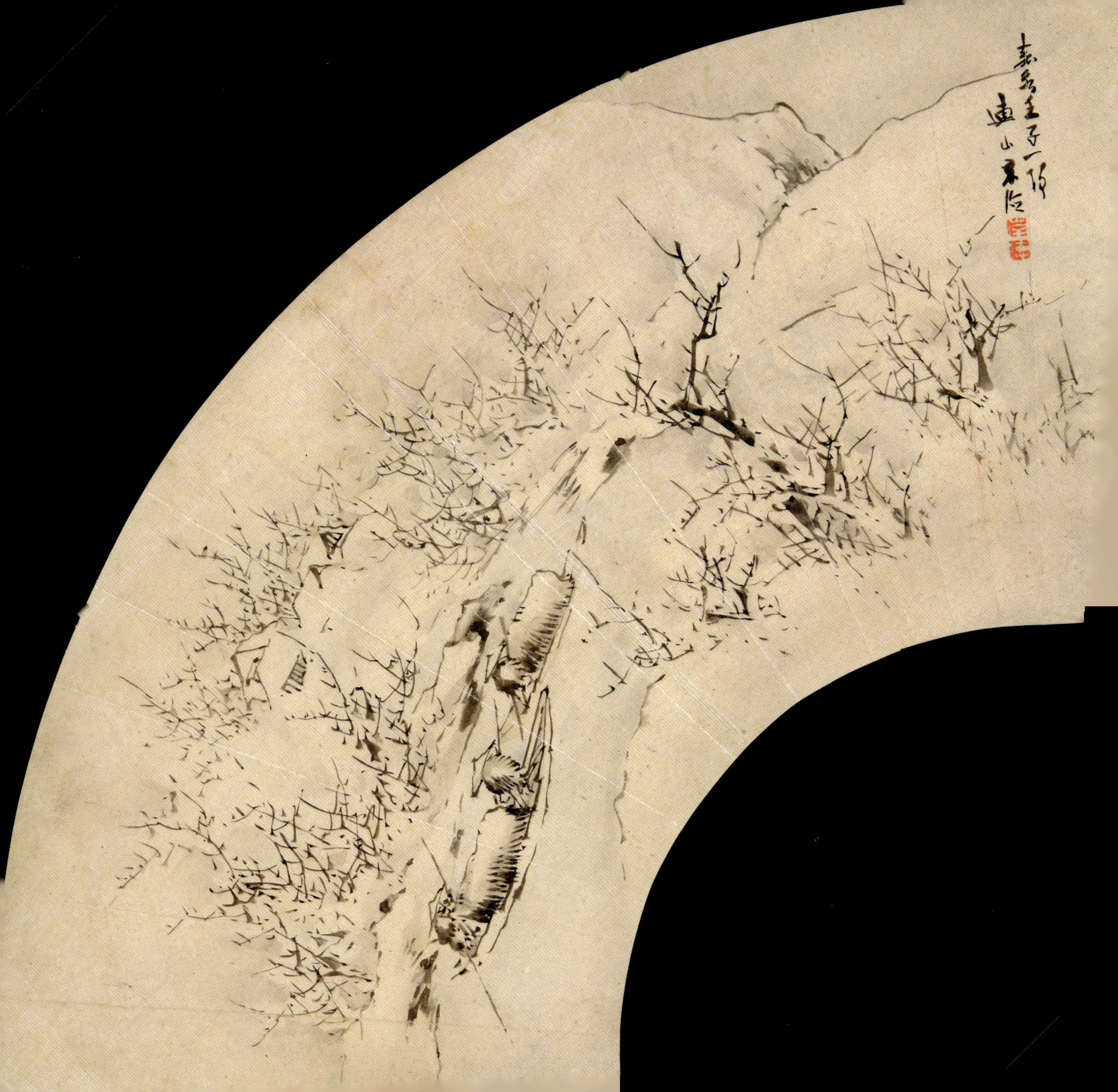
嘉永壬子一陽
連山畫之

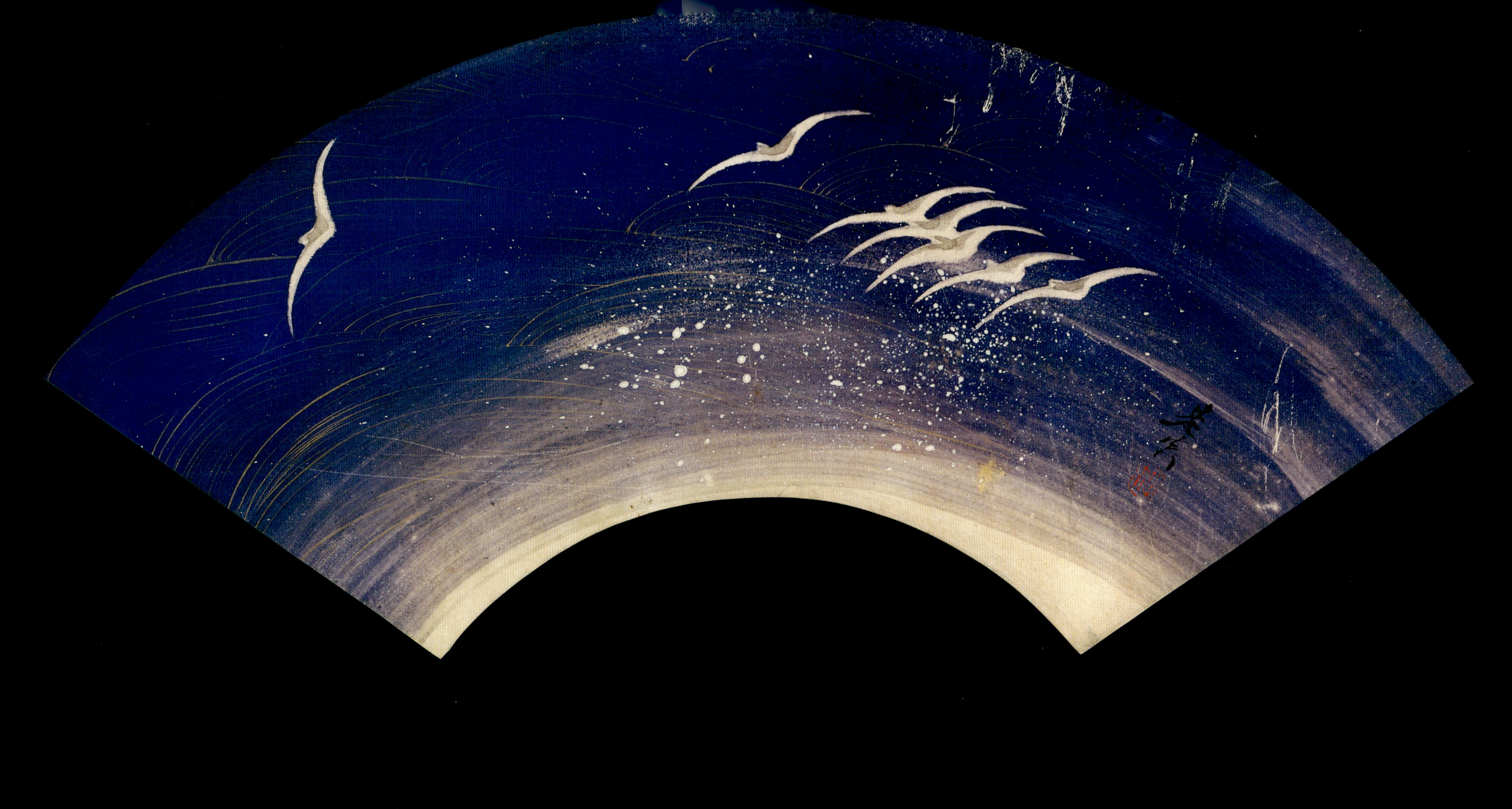

53   Shibata Zeshin, *Pine Trees in the Gorge*

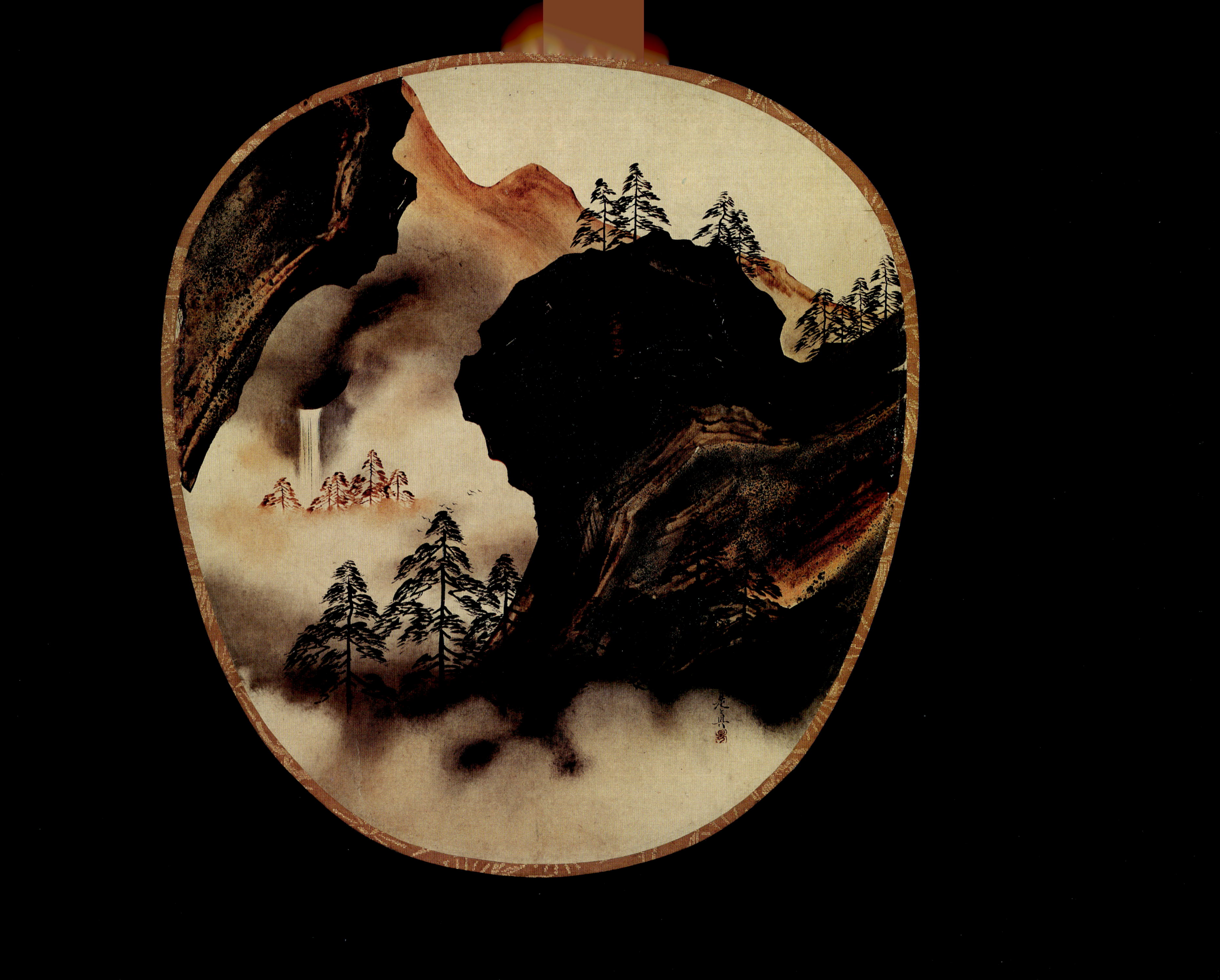

Measurements, exclusive of mountings, are given in centimeters, height preceding width. All Japanese names are rendered in the traditional Japanese manner, with surname preceding given name. Unless otherwise noted, the fans illustrated in this book have been mounted flat as album leaves and are exhibited framed in the Western manner.

RIMPA

1   School of Tawaraya Sōtatsu   17th century
Screen with Fan-shaped Paintings
Six-fold screen, ink and color on paper, 157 x 359 cm.
Seal: Inen
Edwin Janss collection

Published: Yamane Yūzō, ed., *Rimpa kaiga zenshū* (Tokyo, 1977-80), vol. 1, no. 20.

A member of the wealthy merchant class of Kyoto, Sōtatsu maintained a painting atelier called the Tawaraya in Kyoto. It was once believed that the shop specialized in fan paintings, but there is evidence that the Tawaraya dealt in a broader range of art. Nevertheless, there are a number of screens extant associated with Sōtatsu with fans either attached to or painted directly on the surface. Here the glittering background of gold and silver represents stylized sand banks and water. The 36 fans appear to be scattered haphazardly, most of them fully extended but some only halfway open or closed. The resulting irregular rhythm recalls blossoms or leaves scattered by the wind.

The subject matter of the individual fan paintings is very traditional; the flowers, grasses and six poets are all classical Heian period themes and show the revived interest in *yamato-e* in Kyoto during the Edo period. One poet is represented on each panel, and they are as follows: Tomonori, Motora, Toshinari, Ietaka, Narihira, and Toshiyori. The combination of poets with seasonal flowers and plants is indicative of the strong bond between poetry and painting in Japan.

2   Ogata Kōrin   1658-1716
Utsunoyama Scene from Tale of Ise
Round fan, ink, color and gold on gesso, 35.6 x 22.7 cm.
Signature: Hokkyō Kōrin   Seal: Kansei
Seal: Kansei
Freer Gallery of Art, Smithsonian Institution, Washington, D.C., 03.1 (not in exhibition)

Published: *Masterpieces of Chinese and Japanese Art: Freer Gallery of Art Handbook* (Washington, D.C., 1976), pl. 131; *The Freer Gallery of Art: II Japan* (Tokyo, 1972), no. 50; Yamane Yūzō, ed., *Rimpa kaiga zenshū* (Tokyo, 1977-80), vol. 3, pl. 26-27; *Zaigai Nihon no shihō* (Tokyo, 1979), vol. 5, pls. 60-61.

A master at design in all formats, Kōrin particularly excelled in round fan compositions. This interest may have been sparked by his activities in the family textile business in Kyoto, where he spent long hours creating designs to fit within circles. Some scholars believe that Kōrin's basic approach to composition was to work from a circle and to employ successive circular movements, even in his large-scale paintings.

By their very function, fans would often be gently twisted and rotated so that both sides were visible. Artists would occasionally paint both surfaces, exemplified by this masterpiece in the Freer Gallery. On one side Kōrin has depicted the episode from the *Tale of Ise* where two courtiers encountered a wandering ascetic as they passed through Mt. Utsu. Adapting his design to the round format of the fan, Kōrin placed the figures in a triangular pattern which leads the eye around the circle. The simple arrangement is enhanced by the diagonally placed hillocks forming rather complex crisscross patterns which both connect and separate the figures. On the reverse (not illustrated), rolling hills are supplanted by a view of chrysanthemums growing beside a bright blue river.

3   Ogata Kōrin   1658-1716
Autumnal Ivy Leaves with Bamboo
Hanging scroll, ink, color and silver on paper, 22.7 x 28.2 cm.
Seal: Kōrin
Sansō collection

Published: Takamizawa Mokuhansha, *Kōrin* (Tokyo, 1940), pl. 121; Tokyo National Museum, *Sōtatsu-Kōrin-ha zuroku* (Tokyo, 1952); Tanaka Ichimatsu, ed., *Kōrin* (Tokyo, 1959), fig. 84; *Kobijutsu* 47 (January 1975), pp. 69, 76, 77; Yamane Yūzō, ed., *Rimpa kaiga zenshū* Tokyo, 1977-1980), vol. 3, no. 173; John Rosenfield, ed., *Song of the Brush* (Seattle, 1979), no. 60.

Plants and flowers arranged in sweeping diagonals were favored motifs in the paintings of Rimpa masters. This fan by Kōrin is no exception. Although the small format makes the scene more intimate, the two diagonally opposed sections of ivy leaves and bamboo create a boldly asymmetrical design. The coloring is rather subtle, with soft greens and pinks blended into gray tones of ink. In some areas colors were added to a surface still wet with ink, a technique known as *tarashikomi* which forms lovely blurred textures where the ink and pigments have puddled.

4   Ogata Kōrin   1658-1716
Spider
Ink and colors on paper, 14.8 x 46 cm.
Signature: Seisei Kōrin
Seal: Hōshuku
Mr. and Mrs. Leighton R. Longhi collection

Published: *Kōrin gasei nihyakunen ki kinen: Kōrin zuroku* (n.d.), unpaginated; Shirata Yoshi, ed., *Rimpa kaiga zenshū* (Kyoto, 1976), vol. 2, no. 20; Yamane Yūzō, ed., *Rimpa kaiga zenshū* (Tokyo, 1977-80), vol. 3, no. 167.

This rare example of a folding fan by Kōrin outside Japan is especially interesting because of the unusual subject matter. A brown spider dangles down from his web which is attached conspicuously between the branch and trunk of an old tree. The design of the tree, with a large forceful trunk extending out of the picture plane and a branch sweeping diagonally down into another part of the composition, is not unlike that popularized by Kanō painters during the Momoyama period. However, here the scale is much smaller, and Kōrin has further tamed the tree by using soft washes of ink and color instead of rough, angular brushstrokes. The resulting picture is smooth and harmonious, a mood which is sustained by the restriction of colors to cool greens and browns.

5   Ogata Kenzan   1663-1743
Basket of Flowers and Grasses
Folding fan, ink and color on gold ground, 18.4 x 50 cm.
Signature: Kyōchō Itsumin Shisui Shinsei
Seal: Tōzen
Freer Gallery of Art, Smithsonian Institution, Washington, D.C., 11.318 (not in exhibition)

Published: *Masterpieces of Chinese and Japanese Art: Freer Gallery of Art Handbook* (Washington, D.C., 1976), p. 133; *The Freer Gallery of Art: II Japan* (Tokyo, 1972), no. 51; Yamane Yūzō, ed., *Rimpa kaiga zenshū* (Tokyo, 1977-1980), vol. 4, no. 50.

Kenzan is considered to be one of the most brilliant potters of the Edo period who was also skillful at painting and calligraphy. He was influenced a great deal by the designs of his brother Kōrin, who is heralded as one of the great masters of the decorative Rimpa tradition. Establishing successful centers of pottery production in Kyoto and then Edo, Kenzan turned to painting late in his life after moving to the new capital.

This painting of a woven basket brimming with bell-flowers and grasses reveals the influence of Kōrin in both the subject matter and simplified bold design on gold background. On the reverse side of the fan Kenzan has inscribed the following *waka* poem:

Ka to ieba	Oh flowers!
Senshu nagara ni	Multifarious though you be,
Adanaranu	Fickle be you not!
Iroka ni utsuru	It is only the dewdrops of
Nobe no tsuyu kana	the fields
	That are captivated by your
	beauty.

(Translated by Joseph Seubert)

The poem may allude to an episode in Chapter 10 of the *Tale of Genji* when the prince became despondent after being repeatedly rebuffed by Lady Fujitsubo, whom he had long admired. Dew was often used in Japanese poetry as a metaphor for tears, and here may symbolize Genji's love for Fujitsubo who is represented by flowers.

6   Watanabe Shikō   1683-1755
Waterbirds
Pair of hanging scrolls, ink and light colors on silk, each 30.6 x 34 cm
Seal: Shikō no in (same on both)
Shin'enKan collection

Watanabe Shikō is one of the least understood artists of the Edo period. He began his studies of painting with a Kanō school artist, but later became a pupil of Ogata Kōrin. His own style represents a blend of the two traditions, but also displays naturalistic features. Shikō served as a retainer to Konoe Iehiro at the Imperial court in Kyoto, and may have been influenced by Iehiro's interest in Chinese pharmacology. Iehiro himself painted rather detailed bird and flower studies and may have led Shikō in this direction. Shikō in turn was an inspiration to Maruyama Ōkyo who copied many of Shikō's sketches from life.

This pair of round fan-shaped paintings strikes a delicate balance between decoration and naturalism. The ripples of water are naturalistically rendered, with gradations in tone to suggest depth. The birds and plants are also painted with some degree of accuracy, but the forms have also been stylized so that the overall impression is decorative. This is particularly notable in the positioning of the birds so that they are elegantly silhouetted against the background.

7   Attributed to Fukae Roshū   1699-1757
Utsunoyama
Hanging scroll, ink and colors on paper, 19.3 x 45.7 cm.
The Mary and Jackson Burke collection

Published: Harold P. Stern, *Rimpa* (New York, 1971), pl. 44.

The "Utsunoyama" chapter of the *Tale of Ise*, a tenth century classic consisting of poems interspersed with connecting narrative passages, inspired paintings by many Rimpa artists. This painted fan is attributed to Fukae Roshū, who is perhaps most famous for his six-panel screen of this subject in the Cleveland Museum of Art. Roshū did not study directly under Kōrin, but clearly modeled his style after the great Rimpa master.

In this episode, two courtiers are passing through Mount Utsu on the way to the province of Suruga. The road was dark and overgrown with ivy vines. Suddenly a wandering ascetic appeared whom one of the courtiers recognized. The courtier thereupon wrote out a poem and gave it to the ascetic to deliver to a lady friend in the capital, which is the scene represented in this fan. A typical feature of the Rimpa decorative tradition is the smooth, flowing linework which describes the figures, trees, road and slopes of Mount Utsu. Surrounded by dark green slopes and pine trees, the meeting of the courtier and ascetic is accentuated and the narrative made clear.

8   Nakamura Hōchū   fl. 1790-1818
Screen of Fan Paintings
Two-panel screen, ink and colors on gold, 164.5 x 182 cm.
Signatures: Hōchū sha shi, Hōchū ga shi
Seals: Hō, Hō
Mr. and Mrs. Leighton R. Longhi collection

Published: Nakamura Tanio, *Hōitsu-ha kachō-gafu* (Kyoto, 1979), vol. 4, no. 80.

Hōchū was an especial lover of the fan format and numerous fan paintings by him exist in both Japan and the West. Ten fans have been attached to the gold leaf ground on this two-panel screen. The staggered placement of the five fans per panel shows the Japanese preference for asymmetry. Beginning in the upper right, the subjects represented are as follows: a New Year's dancer, Jurōjin (god of longevity), red plum, dandelion, camellia, viewing the autumn foliage, Hotei, soybeans, an unidentified flower and pine trees. Many of the fans have seasonal connotations, but they do not seem to have been arranged with a chronological order in mind.

The designs featuring flowers and grasses are patterned after Kōrin prototypes. Hōchū never studied directly with the master, but was so inspired by Kōrin's art that he published a book of illustrations that were his own interpretations of Kōrin's designs. Hōchū was comparatively more free and playful with the brush and developed a distinctly personal style of *tarashikomi* wet ink effects.

Hōchū's figure of Hotei in the left panel is also reminiscent of Kōrin, but the other figures seem to have also been influenced by the simplified *haiga* tradition brought to fruition by Yosa Buson in the late eighteenth century. Hōchū, however, simplified forms even further so that there is more emphasis on shape and decorative design. A marvelous example is his fan depicting Jurōjin leaning on the back of a reclining deer, hiding his face behind a round fan.

The forms are so simplified that at first glance it reads as an abstract design. Another characteristic of Hōchū was his use of smooth, rounded outlines of wet wash. The resulting softness adds a toylike dimension to his paintings, but it is handled with such elegance that the result is overwhelmingly decorative.

9   Nakamura Hōchū   fl. 1790-1818
Hollyhocks
Ink and color on paper, 20.7 x 51.4 cm.
Signature: Hōchū sha shi
Seal: Hōchū
Kurt A. Gitter and Millie H. Gitter collection

Published: Yamane Yūzō, ed., *Rimpa kaiga zenshū* (Tokyo, 1977-80), vol. 4, no. 223; Stephen Addiss, et al., *A Myriad of Autumn Leaves: Japanese Art from the Kurt and Millie Gitter Collection* (New Orleans, 1983), no. 12.

Red and white hollyhocks were favored motifs of Rimpa school artists, who delighted in creating decorative designs with the pinwheel-shaped flowers. The fan format was extremely well-suited to this subject since its curved shape in part echoes and in part contrasts with the circular blossoms. Hōchū's contribution to this conventional theme lies in his seemingly playful handling of the brush. He added ample water to his ink and pigments so that they would not be uniformly opaque. For the leaves Hōchū used the technique of repeated application called *tarashikomi* where ink and/or colors are dropped onto still moist surfaces. When the painting dries, the mottled patterns created where the ink and colors pooled add a visually interesting element to the overall design.

10   Nakamura Hōchū   fl. 1790-1818
Poppies
Ink and color on paper, 20.7 x 51.4 cm.
Signature: Hōchū sha shi
Seal: Hōchū
Private collection

Hōchū was fond of painting flowering plants, usually selecting two or three blossoms and enlarging them so that they filled much of the fan surface. The flowers and leaves often extend out of the picture plane, adding a dramatic impact to the design. Hōchū applied supple lines of gray ink around the contours of the poppies which emphasize the billowy quality of the petals. The fluent linework and rounded shapes are particularly suited to the curved fan format. In contrast to the bright red color of one of the poppies, the leaves and bud underneath were painted with light washes of green color subtly blended with ink. The overall decorative effect is heightened by the drops of gold paint which glisten softly in the light.

11   Nakamura Hōchū   fl. 1790-1818
Gourd
Ink and color on paper, 15.2 x 48.2 cm.
Signature: Hōchū
Seal: Hōchū
Private collection

At a first glance this fan painting by Hōchū appears to be unpremeditated. However, the asymmetrical composition was in reality thoughtfully laid out, with the gourd bisecting the fan just to the right of center, balanced by the large leaf at the left. These two elements are visually linked by a curling tendril which adds an interesting diagonal thrust of movement into the empty space at the right.

The asymmetrical design is greatly enriched by the luxuriant ink and color. Hōchū's mastery of the *tarashikomi* technique is everywhere apparent, with light washes of green and gold dripped on to surfaces still wet with ink. Through the remarkable textures embellished with gold, this commonplace vine has been transformed into an extraordinary decorative work of art.

12   Nakamura Hōchū   fl. 1790-1818
Crane
Hanging scroll, ink and color on paper, 23.7 x 47.5 cm.
Signature: Hōchū utsusu
Seal: Hōchū
Mr. and Mrs. James Stein collection

Chinese legends record that cranes were the companions and messengers of Taoist immortals, and like them lived for thousands of years. The sun and water both last for eternity, and therefore are also suggestive of long life. Since the motifs in this fan are all symbols of old age, Hōchū probably painted it for an elderly patron or friend with a wish for his longevity.

Hōchū's genius is apparent in painting these time-honored symbols with his characteristic bold and playful spirit. Placed just to the right of center, the crane gingerly walks along the curved edge of the fan, while sparkling blue waves swirl around his feet. Above the crane's head shines the red orb of the sun bisected by the fan's upper edge. The concept of design is very simple, yet the execution is sophisticated in terms of the arrangement of forms and handling of the brush. With the exception of the sticklike legs of the crane, all of the brushlines are soft and flowing, forming rounded shapes which beautifully complement the halfmoon format of the fan.

13   Sakai Hōitsu   1761-1828
Yatsuhashi
Ink and color on gold ground paper, 17.8 x 55 cm.
Signature: Hōitsu hitsu
Seal: Hōitsu
The Seattle Art Museum, Eugene Fuller Memorial Collection, 59.132

Published: *Japanese Art in the Seattle Art Museum* (Seattle, 1960), no. 172; Sherman Lee, *Japanese Decorative Art* (Cleveland, 1961), no. 91.

Hōitsu was born into a wealthy samurai family in Edo and at an early age immersed himself in the study of literary as well as martial arts. He also showed talent in painting, and after experimenting with various traditions devoted himself to the Rimpa style. Inspired by Kōrin's compositions, Hōitsu contented himself with this somewhat abstract design of irises and bridge which represents a famous episode from the *Tale of Ise*. Several men had set out from the capital to find a place to settle in the provinces, and found their way to a place called Yatsuhashi in Mikawa. It was a spot where the waters of a river branched into eight channels, each with a bridge, and thus it was called Yatsuhashi or "eight bridges." Glancing around at the clumps of irises blooming, one of the men suggested that they compose poems on the subject of a "Traveler's Sentiments," beginning each line with a syllable from the word for iris, *kakitsubata*.

This poetic allusion would have been known to any reasonably educated Japanese. Classical literature and poetry inspired countless works during the Edo period, particularly among artists of the Rimpa school who responded by rendering the traditional subjects with bold, innovative designs.

14   Sakai Hōitsu   1761-1828
Maple Branch
Folding fan, ink and color on paper, 19.1 x 48.2 cm.
Signature: Hōitsu hitsu
Seal: Uge-an
Kurt A. Gitter and Millie H. Gitter collection

Published: *Sakai Hōitsu ten* (Tokyo, 1977), no. 56; Stephen Addiss, et al., *A Myriad of Autumn Leaves: Japanese Art from the Kurt and Millie Gitter Collection* (New Orleans, 1983), no. 13.

It is always interesting to observe the ways in which an artist tailors his design to fit the fan format. Echoing the black lacquer spokes of the fan, Hōitsu has painted a black water ladle thrusting in diagonally from the left edge. From behind the ladle's cup springs forth a maple branch with brilliantly colored scarlet leaves, bending to the right so that it conforms to the shape of the fan. The addition of the saké cup brings forth more specific allusions than merely viewing the autumn foliage for it has been suggested that these motifs refer to the Nō drama "Momijigari." In this play, Taira no Koremochi comes across a maple viewing party while out hunting one day and is invited by a court lady to join the group. After several cups of saké he becomes quite intoxicated and falls asleep, whereupon the woman turns into a demon and attempts to kill him. Warned of the danger by a dream, Koremochi awakes in time and makes his escape.

15   Suzuki Kiitsu   1796-1858
Futami Bay
Hanging scroll, ink and colors on silver ground, 22.2 x 50.8 cm.
Signature: Seisei Kiitsu
Seal: Shukurin
Willard G. Clark collection

This fan painting by Kiitsu on a shimmering silver background is one of his rare *shinkeizu* or "true view paintings." The site depicted is Futami Bay in Ise province, which is famous for two great rocks rising offshore. A straw rope is hung between them, signifying a sacred area where Shintō deities reside, and the two rocks have also come to symbolize conjugal love. In Kiitsu's painting the waves are churning so forcefully that the rope is hardly visible.

Kiitsu included a more peaceful view of these rocks in a travel diary which now only exists in the form of a copy by one of his pupils (collection of the Kyoto University library). The fact that this view is different, and is extremely accurate in depicting the swirling pools of water and crashing waves, suggests that it, too, was based on an actual sketch Kiitsu made during his travels. A number of Edo period artists painted views of native landscape based on sketches they had made, but this practice was highly unusual for a follower of the Rimpa tradition which stressed formal design. While remaining faithful to the original view, Kiitsu's training is evident in the waves which are somewhat stylized, and in his choice of the silver sprinkled paper.

NANGA

16   Yosa Buson   1716-1784
Narrow Road to the Deep North
Ink and color on paper, 18.1 x 48.1 cm.
Signature: Yanan ō Buson
Seals: Chōkō, Shunsei
Kurt A. Gitter and Millie H. Gitter collection

The haiku poet Matsuō Bashō (1644-1694) traveled around Japan extensively in his later years, recording his experiences and the poems he composed along the way. His diary of a trip to northern Japan, entitled the *Oku no hosomichi (Narrow Road to the Deep North)*, became one of the most popular literary works in Japan. It served as inspiration to the great poet-painter Yosa Buson, who late in his life painted scenes from the *Oku no hosomichi* combined with written passages of text in the format of scrolls, screens and fans. These paintings were part of a great revival of interest in Bashō, since it was nearing the 150th anniversary of his death.

The passage Buson has illustrated here is from the beginning section of the *Oku no hosomichi*. Staff in hand, Bashō has just set off on his journey followed by his companion Sora. The figures have been freely sketched in the abbreviated style known as *haiga* which recalls the simplicity of haiku poetry. Buson also added the following segment of Bashō's text.

> Mount Kurokami was visible through the mist in the distance. It was brilliantly white with snow in spite of its name, which means black hair.
>
>> Rid of my hair,
>> I came to Mount Kurokami,
>> On the day we put on
>> Clean summer clothes. (Sora)
>
> My companion's real name is Kawai Sōgorō, Sora being his pen name. He used to live in my neighborhood and help me in such chores as bringing water and firewood. He wants to enjoy the views of Matsushima and Kisagata with me, and also to share with me the hardships of the wandering journey. So he took to the road after taking the tonsure on the very morning of our departure, putting on the black robe of an itinerant priest, and even changing his name to Sōgo, which means Religiously Enlightened. His poem, therefore, is not intended as a mere description of Mount Kurokami. The last two lines, in particular, impress us deeply, for they express his determination to persist in his purpose. (Nobuyuki Yuasa, trans., *Bashō: The Narrow Road to the Deep North and Other Travel Sketches* [Baltimore, 1966], pp. 100-101.)

17 Yosa Buson 1716-1784
Narrow Road to the Deep North
Hanging scroll, ink and light color on paper, 18 x 48.4 cm.
Signature: Buson
Seals: Chōkō, Shunsei
The Mary and Jackson Burke collection

Published: Miyeko Murase, *Japanese Art: Selections from the Mary and Jackson Burke Collection* (New York, 1975), no. 74; Louisa Cunningham, *The Spirit of Place: Japanese Paintings and Prints of the Sixteenth through Nineteenth Centuries* (New Haven, 1984), no. 18.

This fan, with a man gazing out of the window of his tiny thatched hut, depicts another episode from Bashō's *Oku no hosomichi*. On both sides of the hut Buson has written out portions of text from the following section in Bashō's diary:

> There was a huge chestnut tree on the outskirts of this post town, and a priest was living in seclusion under its shade. When I stood there in front of the tree, I felt as if I were in the midst of deep mountains where the poet Saigyō had picked nuts. I took a piece of paper from my bag, and wrote as follows:
>
>> The chestnut is a holy tree, for the Chinese ideograph for chestnut is Tree placed directly below West, the direction of the holy land. The priest Gyōki is said to have used it for his walking stick and the chief support of his house.

> The chestnut by the eaves
> In magnificent bloom
> Passes unnoticed
> By men of this world.
> (Nobuyuki Yuasa, trans., *Bashō: The Narrow Road to the Deep North and Other Travel Sketches* [Baltimore, 1966], pp. 107-108.)

Inspired by the gentle nature of Bashō's words, Buson painted this scene with soft, wet strokes of ink overlaid with colorful blue and pink wash. His extreme economy of line and concentration upon a single image results in a lyrical and penetrating illustration that complements the image evoked in the attending poem. Buson's writing flows so naturally above and around the picture that calligraphy, poetry and painting are inseparable in both composition and content.

18 Kō Fuyō 1722-1784
Landscape
Folding fan, ink and light color on paper, 16.5 x 43.8 cm.
Signature: Kō Mōhyō
Seals: Mō, hyō
Private collection

An intimate friend of the Nanga painter Ike Taiga, Kō Fuyō became most highly regarded as a seal engraver. He studied Confucianism in Kyoto and for a short time served as an instructor to a feudal lord. Like many other Japanese sinophiles, his interest extended to Chinese literati painting. Fuyō's paintings are rather rare and tend to be conservative, faithful renditions of Chinese models.

The brushwork in this landscape is unusually free and impressionistic for the artist. In addition, the composition is rather sparse in comparison with other works by Fuyō. The focus is on the tiny pavilion on a rocky ledge surrounded by verdant mountains. Light washes of color impart a spring-like freshness to this tranquil scene.

19 Ike Taiga 1723-1776
Orchid
Ink on mica-treated paper, 18.5 x 51.6 cm.
Signature: Kashō
Seal: Mumei Taisei
Shōka collection

Taiga is said to have begun his career as an artist at age fourteen when he opened a shop and began selling fans painted in the Chinese manner. He used the *Hasshū gafu,* an eight-volume set of Chinese woodblock pictures, as a modelbook for designs.

Several of the volumes in the *Hasshū gafu* were devoted to plant subjects, and it is likely that Taiga was introduced to the "four gentlemen" themes in part through this painting manual. The Oriental orchid has modest, inconspicuous flowers which emit a delicate fragrance, and it was especially admired by literati because its simple form represented purity.

The orchid was also an appropriate subject for the scholar-amateur artist since the brushstrokes required for the leaves and blossoms are similar to those used in calligraphy. Here Taiga has masterfully arranged the orchid within the fan format: the leaves splay outward from a point just off-center, balanced by the signature just to the left. Two lower leaves echo the bend in the fan, providing a sense of stability. The curvilinear movement of the upper edge of the fan is continued by two long, slender leaves flowing gently to the left. This line of movement is again echoed by the long horizontal stroke in the first character of Taiga's signature.

20 Ike Taiga 1723-1776
Cultivating and Weeding the Fields
Hanging scroll, ink on mica-treated paper, 25.8 x 27.6 cm.
Signature: Mumei
Seal: Ike Mumei in
Sansō collection

Published: *Ikeno Taiga gafu* (Tokyo, 1958), vol. 4, pl. 525; Kurimoto Kazuō, et al., *Ike Taiga sakuhin shū* (Tokyo, 1960), pl. 525; John M. Rosenfield, ed., *Song of the Brush* (Seattle, 1979), no. 41.

Taiga was a master at painting in all formats, from folding screens to small, intimate fans. As though looking out through a porthole, here he has given us a glimpse at a typically Japanese rural scene. Along the border of rice fields in the foreground, a tree powerfully thrusts out its branches. At the right a figure stands underneath a thatched roof porch, watching another man as he crosses the small footbridge. Around them flows a stretch of water which also becomes the sky. In the upper portion of the fan are more rice fields, divided into neat squares by irrigation channels.

The rice paddies above are presumably to be perceived as farther off in the distance, yet there is no real attempt to represent spatial recession. Instead, Japanese artists (and Taiga was no exception) were more interested in the formal elements of design. Taiga has purposely distorted some of the motifs, including the sense of perspective, in order to create a more striking work of art. The paddies become abstract patterns, with dots representing rice plants clustered inside diamond shapes. The foreground tree was rendered with dark brushstrokes resembling bolts of lightning. Taiga's great skill and wit have transformed a charming pastoral scene into a bold and innovative design.

21 Ike Taiga 1723-1776
Landscape with Yellow Trees
Ink and colors on mica-treated paper, 19.5 x 48.4 cm.
Signature: Kashō
Seals: Zenshin sōma Hō Kyūkō, Kashō
Kurt A. Gitter and Millie H. Gitter collection

Published: Stephen Addiss, et al., *A Myriad of Autumn Leaves: Japanese Art from the Kurt and Millie Gitter Collection* (New Orleans, 1983), no. 38.

In contrast to the fan painting in number 20 in which angular lines predominate, in this landscape Taiga employed rounded brushstrokes. This is particularly evident in the trunks and branches of the trees, which here wiggle playfully. The scene is again a peaceful rural one, although no figures are to be seen. The colors have somewhat faded, but pastel shades of green, blue, yellow and yellowish-orange making up the tree foliage suggest that the season intended is autumn. Taiga applied the dots and lines with his characteristic verve, imbuing them with a shimmering vibrancy which is the hallmark of his style.

22 Ike Taiga   1723-1776
Mount Fuji
Ink on mica-treated paper, 18.5 x 51.5 cm.
Signature: Kashō
Seal: Hanchi hankatsu
Fred and Isabel Pollard Collection,
Art Gallery of Greater Victoria, British Columbia

Published: Kurimoto Kazuō, et al., *Ike Taiga sakuhin shū* (Tokyo, 1960), no. 603; John Vollmer and Glenn T. Webb, *Japanese Art at the Art Gallery of Greater Victoria* (Victoria, B.C., 1972), no. 16; Joan Stanley-Baker, *Nanga: Idealist Painting of Japan* (Victoria, B.C., 1980), no. 2; Barry Till, *Japanese Paintings in Canadian Collections* (Victoria, B.C., 1983), no. 45A.

Mount Fuji seems to have held special meaning for Taiga, and his memorial marker states that he climbed the mountain several times. The reasons for making the pilgrimage may have been partially religious, for in the Shugendō mountain-climbing religious sect, Fuji is sacred and inhabited by powerful deities.

Although we know that he made actual sketches of the famous peak, here Taiga has contented himself with outlining Fuji in the conventional manner as seen from a distance. The mountain rises just to the right of the center of the fan, its top divided into three peaks. Gray wash was added to the interior, but some areas of white paper were left to represent snow and clouds. From the bottom edge of the fan in the foreground rises a low slope rendered in darker wash, its shape conforming to the format of the fan. This predilection for curved shapes was somewhat relieved by the straight line of trees in the background and small boat underneath. The final product is a skillful balance of line versus wash, dark versus light, and areas of blank space versus painted areas.

23 Ike Taiga   1723-1776
Country Retreat in Early Summer
Hanging scroll, ink and light color on paper, 18.2 x 50 cm.
Signature: Kashō
Seals: Ka, shō
The Mary and Jackson Burke collection

Published: Kurimoto Kazuō, et al., *Ike Taiga sakuhin shū*

(Tokyo, 1960), no. 292; Miyeko Murase, *Japanese Art: Selections from the Mary and Jackson Burke Collection* (New York, 1975), no. 71.

The dancing rhythm of Taiga's brushwork is clearly evident in this painted fan which is now mounted as a hanging scroll. The compositional design is very full, with trees, rocks and mountains spread out over the entire surface. The landscape curves to fit within the fan shape instead of adhering to the conventional horizon line.

The lush foliage indicates that the season is summer, as does the addition of light green color washes. However, the feeling of tranquility induced by the solitary figure walking across the bridge at the left, and cool breezes suggested by the presence of the lake, make this the perfect scene to view while fanning oneself on a hot, sultry day.

24 Ike Gyokuran   1727 or 1728-1820
Sojourning Guests in a Bamboo Grove
Ink and color on paper, 15.8 x 44 cm.
Signature: Gyokuran
Seal: undecipherable
Inscription: see text below
Private collection

The wife of the great painter Ike Taiga, Gyokuran was an accomplished poet and painter in her own right. As a young woman, she had helped to operate a teahouse in the Gion district of Kyoto which had been established by her grandmother and consequently passed on to her mother. Gyokuran's mother and grandmother were also well-known poets and they are collectively referred to as the "three women of Gion."

Gyokuran frequently inscribed her paintings with verses by her mother or herself. Here she has written out a *waka* by the poet and scholar of Japanese studies, Chikage (1735-1808), which reads:

Kuretake no	Over the black bamboo
Yukage mo yoshi	The light of the setting sun
Sunao naru	Gently fades away—
Yo no furugoto mo	We reminisce about the past
Katariakasan	All night long

To complement the poem, Gyokuran painted two men huddled in conversation beneath swaying stalks of bamboo. The figure types are Chinese and recall the seated scholars often painted by Taiga. The ultimate model for this theme may have been the "Seven Sages of the Bamboo Grove," a group of third century Chinese scholars who withdrew from society to the seclusion of a bamboo grove and devoted themselves wholeheartedly to literati pursuits.

25 Ike Gyokuran   1727 or 1728-1820
Landscape
Hanging scroll, ink and color on paper, 23.8 x 52.3 cm.
Signature: Gyokuran
Seal: Gyokuran

The Metropolitan Museum of Art, New York, The Harry G. C. Packard Collection of Asian Art, Gift of Harry G. C. Packard and Purchase, Fletcher, Rogers, Harris Brisbane Dick, and Louis V. Bell Funds, Joseph Pulitzer Bequest and The Annenberg Fund, Inc. Gift, 1975. (1975.268.95)

Gyokuran learned painting from her husband Ike Taiga, who is noted for his Japanization of the Chinese painting tradition known as Nanga or *bunjinga*. Taiga reduced textures to flat patterns, and the surface quality of his paintings is reminiscent of pointillism. Gyokuran continued in this vein, but transformed his style so that her images took on an even more decorative and abstract quality.

In this landscape Gyokuran has obviously strayed far from the organic forms of mountains, rocks and trees. The wavering, ropelike strokes describing the mountains have taken on a life of their own, and the dots applied with more concern for the overall balance and rhythm than for representing foliage. The resulting rich textural surface has a quality akin to woven tapestry, and reveals the Japanese love of converting the world around them into elements of design.

26 Ike Gyokuran   1727 or 1728-1820
Akashi Bay
Hanging scroll, ink on mica-treated paper, 17.5 x 45 cm.
Signature: Gyokuran
Seal: Shōfū, Gyokuran
Shōka collection

Published: *Poem Paintings* (London, 1977), no. 11.

Poetry and painting are more closely united in Asia than anywhere else in the world, a fact which is well represented by this lovely fan painted and inscribed by Ike Gyokuran. Her poem written out in fluid *kana* script reads:

Akashigata	On Akashi Bay
Koyoi no tsuki no	This evening's moon is
Kage kiyoku	Glittering brightly—
Namiji harukeri	Boats far out at sea
Fune zo kogi yuku	Are rowing away.

(Translated by Stephen Addiss)

In the upper right two boats can be seen, and lower down three horizontal spits of land covered with pine trees extend into Akashi Bay. The painted forms are rendered with great brevity, complementing the simple linework of Gyokuran's calligraphy. A balance is struck by the concentration of landscape elements on the right and poem on the left, although in the center of the fan Gyokuran's writing slightly overlaps the pine trees. Just to the left of center is the character for "moon" which from its positioning above the pine trees can also be read as a pictorial image, showing that the poem and paintings are inextricably woven together in terms of content and design. Gyokuran's impression of Akashi Bay at night is enhanced by the choice of paper treated with mica, which shimmers softly as though lit by moonlight.

27 Ki Baitei   1734-1810
Three Riders in the Rain
Hanging scroll, ink and light color on paper, 18 x 50.7 cm.
Signature: Kyūrō sha su
Seals: Bai, tei
Private collection

Published: Cal French, et al., *The Poet-Painters: Buson and His Followers* (Ann Arbor, 1974), no. 24.

Baitei was one of the two outstanding pupils of Yosa Buson. Leaving Kyoto in the 1780s, he moved to the nearby city of Ōtsu along the shores of Lake Biwa. There Baitei became extremely successful as a local artist, and he was responsible for keeping the Buson tradition alive and popular in that region. Although Baitei's early works were based closely on his master's style, his later works such as this fan represent a personal interpretation of the Buson tradition. Baitei's brushwork is often very powerful and dynamic, and his compositions are simplified with forms pared down to geometric shapes.

The three riders plodding slowly toward the left provide a strong sense of lateral movement which echoes the horizontal format of this fan. Its gentle curve is reinforced by the rounded rocks in the foreground and the mountains which rise in the distance. Baitei used ink that was highly saturated with water to paint the surrounding landscape so that all natural forms appear veiled by the gray misty atmosphere. Nebulous ink effects were also achieved by using mica-treated paper which does not absorb ink rapidly, instead allowing it to pool and create interesting blurred textures evocative of fog. Gray ink washes predominate, but any feeling of gloom is washed away by the fresh pink and green colors and the soft, shimmering mica.

28 Satake Kaikai   1738-1790
Traveling Through Cold Mountains
Ink on paper, 23 x 51 cm.
Signature: Kai Kai shūmin
Seals: Teikichi (Sadakichi); second seal undecipherable
Inscription: same as title
British Museum

Published: Milne Henderson, *Nanga Fan Painting* (London, 1975), no. 6.

Born into a family of saké merchants in Kyoto, Kaikai chose to devote himself to the study of Chinese literati painting and poetry. He became a pupil of Ike Taiga and developed a style based on the master's. Unable to make a living as an artist, Kaikai eventually returned to the family business, but still continued to be active in Kyoto literati circles.

Kaikai inscribed this work with the four-character title "Traveling Through Cold Mountains" which closely resembles Taiga's buoyant calligraphy. Underneath, two horsemen move along a path to the left, followed by a man leading what appears to be a bull. Steep mountains rise at both the left and right, embracing the central figures who are also enclosed in a tiny space cell demarcated by three clumps of trees. Kaikai rendered the entire composition in ink, and his emphasis on linear brushwork imparts a patterned, almost printed quality to the painting. The striated texture strokes forming the mountains were clearly derived from Taiga, as is the technique of painting trees and figures with broken rather than continuous lines. Nevertheless, the rhythm of the brushstrokes is somewhat different, indicative of Kaikai's individualistic personality.

29 Okada Beisanjin   1744-1820
Landscape
Folding fan, ink on paper, 17.5 x 48.2 cm.
Signature: Nanjūgo Beiō ga (Painted by seventy-five year old Beiō)
Seal: Beisanjin
Inscription: The road to the eastern river is a thousand *li,*
              It is difficult to move my aged body forward.
              Leisurely I put myself amidst the painting,
              And accompany you across to a scenic spot.
Museum of Fine Arts, Boston, 1973.106, Marshall H. Gould Fund

This work was painted near the end of Beisanjin's career when he had achieved great fame as an artist. Originally a rice merchant, Beisanjin studied Chinese philosophy and poetry and later served as a Confucian scholar in the Tsu fief (present-day Mie prefecture). His interest in Chinese studies also led him to explore the world of literati painting. Although Beisanjin modeled his style upon Chinese literati masters, he developed a very individualistic brush manner featuring bold and swift strokes. His landscapes are often dominated by pine trees with long, slender trunks and the conical shaped mountains seen here. In the center of the fan, a scholar on horseback followed by his servant carrying a *ch'in* can be seen moving toward the clustered buildings at the left. The red flag flying from the extended pole marks one of the huts as a wine shop. This painting perfectly exemplifies the ideals of the literatus who sought solace in the tranquility of nature and the harmony attained through wine and the company of good friends.

30 Uragami Gyokudō   1745-1820
Lingering Rain in a Mountain Hamlet
Hanging scroll, ink on paper, 16.6 x 47.9 cm.
Signature: Gyokudō
Seals: Hakuzen kinshi, Kinsen
Inscription: Lingering Rain in the Half of the Hamlet
The Mary and Jackson Burke collection (not in exhibition)

Published: Miyake Kyūnosuke, *Uragami Gyokudō shinseki shū (Tokyo, 1955)*, I, pl. 28; Tokyo National Museum, ed., *Nihon no bunjinga ten* (Tokyo, 1965), no. 200; Okayama Museum, ed., *Uragami Gyokudō to sono jidai* (Okayama, 1970), no pl. no.; Suzuki Susumu, "Hamlet in Lingering Rain," *Kobijutsu* 30 (June 1970), p. 127; Miyeko Murase, *Japanese Art: Selections from the Mary and Jackson Burke Collection* (New York, 1977), no. 77; Tanaka Ichimatsu, et al., *Uragami Gyokudō gafu* (Tokyo, 1979), vol. 2, no. 124.

Mountain landscapes are extremely well-suited to the fan medium since the rounded forms of the peaks rhythmically echo the curved shape of the paper. Here Gyokudō has typically brushed a row of trees in the foreground. In the center, a tiny scholar can be seen traversing a bridge, his body hunched over as though it, too, were conforming to the bend in the fan. Narrow spits of land extending in from both the left and right provide a welcome contrast to the predominate curved forms. Beyond them rise several layers of mountains, rendered with short, horizontal brushstrokes. Some areas are almost totally obliterated by bands of mist, and the overall atmosphere is damp and hazy.

Gyokudō's interest in nature was nurtured during his years of travel after he resigned his official post in 1794. He became a master at expressing nature in flux, a theme which is also apparent in his poetry. Experimenting with repetitions of both forms and brushwork, Gyokudō built up rhythms which make his mountains and trees vibrate with life.

31 Uragami Gyokudō   1745-1820
Spring Clouds Like Thick Paste
Hanging scroll, ink and light color on silk, 27.6 cm. (diameter)
Signature: Gyokudō
Seal: Suikyō
Kurt A. Gitter and Millie H. Gitter collection

Published: *Kobijutsu* 34 (1971); Tanaka Ichimatsu, et al., *Gyokudō gafu* (Tokyo, 1979), vol. 3, no. 230; Stephen Addiss, et al., *A Myriad of Autumn Leaves: Japanese Art from the Kurt and Millie Gitter Collection* (New Orleans, 1983), no. 57.

In his last years, Gyokudō turned more and more to smaller formats for painting, sometimes deliberately limiting the space for his compositions by drawing outlines in varied geometric shapes. Here he first brushed a rather misshapen circle, perhaps recalling the round format used initially for Chinese fans. One of the effects of compressing his landscapes into such small spaces is that the energetically brushed forms seem ready to burst beyond their confines. This emphasizes even more the strength and dynamism of Gyokudō's brushwork.

The motifs apparent in such mature landscapes as this one were tirelessly repeated by Gyokudō, who was striving to express the rhythms he felt existed in nature. There is a naturalness and freedom in Gyokudō's brushwork which imbues his landscapes with a sense of spontaneous growth.

32 Kuwayama Gyokushū   1746-1799
Landscape
Ink and colors on paper, 18.2 x 49 cm.
Signature: Kuwa Shisan
Seals: Gyoku, shū
Shōka collection

Published: Milne Henderson, *Nanga Fan Painting*
   (London, 1975), no. 8.

Born into a wealthy merchant family in Wakayama, Gyokushū later befriended the Nanga painter Ike Taiga and became his pupil. Certain features of Taiga's style are evident in Gyokushū's painting, such as the flat patterning of texture strokes, but Gyokushū's works lack the playful exuberance of his teacher.

Here Gyokushū clustered a group of huts amidst peaks at the right; mountains, trees and buildings seem to grow right out of the bottom edge of the fan. The bird's eye view and technique of cutting off forms provide us with a more intimate view. The world of man slowly gives way to nature, and the left half of the fan is almost solely devoted to mountains formed with wet ink and color washes. The tooth-like configuration of the jagged peaks originally would have been enhanced greatly by the folds of the fan. The balance between detailed sections and blank space is masterfully handled, imparting a mood of calm and stability.

33 Kameda Bōsai   1752-1826
In My Leisure, 1823
Folding fan, ink and color on paper, 18.2 x 50 cm.
Signature: Bōsai Rōjin suiga
Seals: Chōkō no in, Bokuno, Bōsai
Inscription: (see below)
Private collection

Published: Stephen Addiss, *The World of Kameda Bōsai:
   The Calligraphy, Poetry, Painting and Artistic Circle of a
   Japanese Literatus* (New Orleans, 1984), no. 53.

This folding fan, still in its original format, is one of Bōsai's last landscapes, inscribed as painted at the age of 72. Bōsai led an eventful life, metamorphosing from a Confucian scholar to an artistic wanderer to a free lance literatus. When the government denounced his type of Confucianism and his pupils began to quit his academy, Bōsai turned his back on the world and devoted himself to painting, poetry, calligraphy and travel. His art advanced considerably, and Bōsai's poems and paintings express very directly and modestly his personal feelings toward life and nature.

This work represents a true blending of painting, poetry and calligraphy. Half of the surface is taken over by Bōsai's poetic inscription, written in the dancing cursive script for which he is famous. At the right, a scholar can be seen crossing a bridge. The pavilion perched atop the rocky cliff was also a symbol of the scholarly recluse, and indeed this fan painting calls forth longings for the peace and serenity in nature.

In my leisure, I sleep beside the lovers' trees,
Or row out among the intertwined lotus flowers.
Why does the wild goose come to these sand islands?
For whom does he labor to fly so far?
   (translated by Stephen Addiss)

34 Tani Bunchō   1763-1840
River and Willows, 1800
Ink on paper, 23 x 49.7 cm.
Signature: Bunchō
Seals: Bun, Chō
Inscription: Painted in 1800, the 22nd day of the second
             month; a view of Chiangnan after rain
British Museum

Published: Milne Henderson, *Nanga Fan painting*
   (London, 1975), no. 28; Carol Dorrington-Ward, ed.,
   Fans from the East (New York, 1978), no. 17.

In the right hand portion of this fan, willow trees dripping with moisture bend solemnly over a river bank. To simulate the desired misty effect, Bunchō used wet strokes of ink to define the leaves. The images were blurred by the addition of more water, evoking the feeling of a riverview enveloped in fog at dawn or dusk. Only a hint of the far bank can be seen in the upper left, and a great deal of the fan surface was left blank to denote the large expanse of water. A fishing boat drifts into the upper left corner, poled by long, narrow poles which form a small X. The overall mood is one of solitude and tranquility, qualities that were sought after by literati in both China and Japan.

Bunchō inscribed this work as being a view of Chiangnan, an area in South China which includes the cities of Hangchou, Suchou and Wu-hsing. Famed for its beautiful scenery and gardens, this region has a long tradition of culture and art, and it was frequented by both painters and poets. Bunchō himself did not travel to China, but was probably inspired by Chinese paintings or woodblock prints of this subject. Nevertheless, his highly asymmetrical composition is unique and displays Bunchō's skill early in his career in recreating the lush wet scenery of a riverbank in mist.

35 Tani Bunchō   1763-1840
Landscape, 1808
Ink and colors on paper, 36 x 55 cm. (card mount)
Signature: Bunchō
Seal: Shazan
Inscription: Painted in the autumn of the Dragon year, 1808
The Ashmolean Museum

Published: Jack Hillier, *The Harari Collection of Japanese
   Paintings and Drawings* (London, 1973), vol. 3, no. 303;
   Carol Dorrington-Ward, ed., *Fans from the East* (New
   York, 1878), no. 18.

Tani Bunchō was one of the most prolific artists of his time, adept at painting in an astonishing diversity of styles. He reportedly had multitudes of pupils and was one of the great leaders in Edo artistic world. Although many of his paintings are inconsistent with the literati concept, Bunchō is usually classified as a Nanga painter.

This painted fan, done when Bunchō was in his early 40s, well represents his interest in the Chinese scholar-amateur tradition. In the lower left, a scholar followed by a servant carrying his *ch'in* is making his way to the buildings at the far right. Surrounded by mountains floating amidst the mist and clouds, the mood is one of tranquility and harmony with nature. Unlike the works of his later years, Bunchō's brushwork here is delicate and restrained. The addition of soft, pastel colors imparts a springlike freshness to the scene.

36 Yokoi Kinkoku   1763-1832
Landscape
Ink and light color on paper, 17.9 x 47.5 cm.
Signature: Kinkoku
Seal: Kinkoku
Kurt A. Gitter and Millie H. Gitter collection

Painted with the speed and violence of a storm, a group of trees thrust inward from rocky cliffs at the right. To the left, steep mountains rise sharply with unusual angular, faceted surfaces. In the center a small figure sits within his hut, seemingly oblivious to the torrential display of nature's forces all around him. The contrast between the sense of tranquility and inner peace of the man in the hut and the raging landscape is startlingly bold, and reflects the unique vision of Yokoi Kinkoku.

Kinkoku was ordained as a priest in the Jōdo sect of Buddhism, but spent the second half of his life as a wandering ascetic and follower of the mountain-climbing religious sect called Shugendō. He made religious pilgrimages to mountains all over Japan, experiencing wild, untamed nature which he felt compelled to express with brush and ink. His paintings were thought to embody some of the mystical powers of spirits living the mountains he had climbed, and served as talisman pictures to ward off evil and invite good luck. This is the only known fan painting by Kinkoku; despite its small format, the vitality of nature is powerfully communicated by his kinetic brushwork.

37 Nakabayashi Chikutō   1776-1853
Lofty Recluse Amidst Streams and Mountains
Hanging scroll, ink and color on paper, 18 x 49.5 cm.
Signature: Chūtan
Seals: Chiku, tō
Inscription: same as title
Shōka collection

The four character title that Chikutō added to this delicately composed fan painting succinctly describes the scene: a scholar sits in his thatched hut, looking out upon the marvelous view of a mountain stream cascading down over the rocky cliff to the left. Although evocative of nature, in Chikutō's brushwork the landscape was transformed into decorative patterns. Circular areas of dotted foliage spin like pinwheels, set off boldly against the surrounding squared-off rocks. The water was rendered by leaving blank areas of paper around the rocks; this combined with the ample space around each brushstroke creates a feeling of shimmering lightness.

Chikutō was one of the most outstanding third generation Nanga masters, who advocated a return to orthodox Chinese literati models. Compared to his Japanese Nanga predecessors, Chikutō's landscapes are more carefully constructed and were depicted with more restraint. However, the directness of design and clarity of brushwork distinguishes them as Japanese. The light washes of peach and blue color add a sunny warmth to this intimate scene. With his characteristic restraint and elegance, Chikutō has admirably expressed the feeling of serenity and harmony with nature that scholars sought to convey.

38 Nukina Kaioku   1778-1863
Landscape with Pines, 1825
Ink and color on paper, 15.4 x 46.3 cm.
Signature: Kaioku sei
Seals: Zōteki; Nukina Kummo
Inscription: see text below
Private collection

Nukina Kaioku was renowned as a teacher of Confucian studies as well as for his painting and calligraphy. The son of a samurai from Tokushima on the island of Shikoku, he was so eager to learn painting that he went to the port city of Nagasaki to study with Hidaka Tetsuō (1791-1871). Kaioku eventually moved to Kyoto where he established his own academy.

Landscape with Pines is one of Kaioku's earliest extant works. Kaioku has arranged the mountain landscape so that it bends with the shape of the fan, the pine trees providing strong verticals to offset the horizontality. The squared-off mountain and rock forms are painted with a very dry brush which, combined with the light touches of green wash, well express a crisp, cold day. Kaioku inscribed upon the fan an earlier poem suggesting man's unity with nature.

Pines purify a man's ears—the melody is divine and majestic.
Mountains block out the worldly, forming a green wall.
Waking the servant boy to pick food for the cranes,
I open my brocade book of the Taoist classics.

Painted in 1825, during the rainy season, to record an old poem.

39 Okada Hankō   1782-1846
Landscape
Folding fan, ink on paper, 17.5 x 48.2 cm.
Signature: Hankō Denshuku
Seal: Hankō

Inscription: For a myriad seasons—mountain colors,
        For thousands of years—the sound of water.
        Amidst the clouds and among the pines,
        Cranes come to visit the avowed hermit.
Following Yeh Dan-nien's painting, from the southern window of Jitekisai.
Museum of Fine Arts, Boston, 1973.107,
Marshall H. Gould Fund

Hankō inherited his father Beisanjin's position as a Confucian scholar serving the Tsu fief, but later in life retired to Osaka where he dedicated himself to the study of poetry and art. As a child he was taught painting by his father, but Hankō's mature style as seen here is distinctly more delicate and refined. Hankō followed the trend of other 19th century Nanga artists who turned back to orthodox Chinese masters for inspiration.

In this fan, Hankō's fondness for the Chinese-derived blue and green tradition is evident; he frequently added rich color washes to his paintings which gives them a popular appeal. Here Hankō has focused on a sage seated cross-legged in an open thatched hut, peacefully watching herons alight in the tall grasses surrounding the nearby pond.

40 Yamamoto Baiitsu 1783-1856
Pine Trees
Hanging scroll, ink and light color on mica-treated paper, 14.3 x 46.7 cm.
Signature: Baiitsu
Seal: Ryō
Shōka collection

Baiitsu was a member of a group of artists active in the area of Nagoya and Kyoto who advocated fidelity to the Chinese literati painting tradition. By the early nineteenth century more actual Chinese paintings were available in Japan for study, and Baiitsu's generation believed that these were the proper models to emulate. Compared with earlier Japanese Nanga, Baiitsu's paintings exhibit such sinophile features as systematized layering of brushstrokes and traditional compositional schemes.

Since pine trees were symbols of longevity, it is likely that Baiitsu painted this work for an elderly friend or patron. Now mounted as a hanging scroll, it was actually used at one time as a folding fan. The concentration of trees and rocks on the left is balanced nicely by the open space to the right. The pine boughs form a mushroom shape which follows the curve of the fan. The treetops are cut off by the upper edge of the fan, but this only emphasizes their height and in no way decreases the grandeur of these venerable pines. Although the composition is somewhat sparse, Baiitsu's brushwork is rich and varied, displaying his personal blending of wet and dry strokes.

41 Watanabe Kazan   1793-1841
Night Rain on the Hsiao and Hsiang, 1840
Ink on paper, 16.6 x 50.8 cm.
Seal: Noboru
Inscription: Painted in 1840, the end of the eighth month,
        on the 24th day, following Chao Sung-hsüeh's idea
Private collection

Watanabe Kazan is well-known in Japan, for in addition to being a scholar, poet and painter, he became a national hero. He was imprisoned in 1838 because of his criticism of Shogunate policies and dedication to Western learning. The initial death sentence was changed to permanent house arrest, but three years later Kazan committed suicide.

Kazan's early interest in painting led him to study with Tani Bunchō in Edo. In addition to studying the Nanga and Nagasaki traditions, he also learned to paint in the realistic Western style. This fan painting of bamboo reflects Kazan's scholarly nature: the slender stalks were brushed with ink in the traditional literati manner. According to the four-character title, this represents one of the eight famous views of the Hsiao and Hsiang river regions in China. The Chinese paintings of this subject that inspired earlier Japanese versions generally feature overall landscapes, rendered with soft, suggestive ink washes. However, like Ike Taiga's famous set of Hsiao and Hsiang fans, Kazan has boldly simplified the view, leaving more to the viewer's imagination. Kazan wrote in his inscription that he was following the Yuan dynasty scholar-painter Chao Meng-fu's conception. Chao Meng-fu was highly regarded in literati circles as a painter of bamboo, and he was an important figure in establishing the concept that painting was similar to calligraphy and hence an appropriate pastime for the scholar.

42 Watanabe Kazan   1793-1841
Portrait of Kō Sūkoku
Folding fan, ink, color, gold and silver on paper, 17.8 x 45.7 cm.
Signature: Watanabe Noboru sha   Seal: Noboru
Inscription: A small portrait of Kō Sūkoku
The Cleveland Museum of Art, Purchase, James Parmelee Fund, 76.8

Published: "Kazan no chimpin nidai," *Geijutsu shincho,* 1976, no. 4; Sherman E. Lee, "Varieties of Portraiture in Chinese and Japanese Art," *The Bulletin of the Cleveland Museum of Art,* vol. 64 (April, 1977), figs. 16, 17; Sherman E. Lee, et al., *Reflections of Reality in Japanese Art* (Cleveland, 1983), no. 122; James T. Ulak, "Kazan's Portrait of a Giant: Ozorabuzaemon," *The Bulletin of the Cleveland Museum of Art,* vol. 70, no. 3 (March, 1983), p. 101.

Portraits painted on fans are highly unusual; the circumstances surrounding the creation of this one illustrate that Nanga artists in particular regarded the fan as more intimate and personal than other formats. The subject is the Edo artist Kō Sūkoku (1730-1804). It was painted by Watanabe Kazan as a kind of memorial, perhaps on an anniversary of Sūkoku's death. On the reverse side of the fan is a poem written out by Tani Bunchō which seems to be a variation on Sūkoku's final haiku poem.

> The grave is readied
> And the saké warmed.
> Ah, the cold.
> (Translated by James Ulak)

Bunchō instructed Kazan in painting and was likely a friend of Sūkoku as well. When Sūkoku died, Kazan was only 11 years old, which suggests that the two may never have met. In painting this portrait Kazan probably relied upon available sketches and advice from his teacher Bunchō. Kazan was clearly fascinated with techniques of verisimilitude which he learned from imported Chinese and European art works. Here he has rendered Sūkoku's visage with great sensitivity, using primarily line but also light color washes for interior modeling. Kazan enclosed the portrait within a circle of golden wash as though Sūkoku were a religious figure, indicating his great respect for the deceased artist.

43 Haruki Nanmei   1795-1878
Summoning a Ferry on the Autumn River
Ink and color on paper, 14.7 x 45.4 cm.
Signature: Nanmei
Seal: undecipherable
Private collection

Framed by two trees in the center, a peasant wearing a straw hat calls out to the ferry boat at the far right. He may well have just come from the old thatched hut at the left, enclosed by waving stalks of bamboo. The river divides the scene into two equal parts, creating a feeling of tranquility. A peaceful mood is also evoked by the choice of blue and green washes to color the hillsides. Such plebian, rural scenes were a common subject in the literati painting tradition as they represented the ideal of living in harmony with nature.

A resident of Edo, Nanmei was the son of the well-known painter, Haruki Nanko (1759-1839). In addition to studying with his father, Nanmei also became a pupil of the leading Nanga artist in Edo at the time, Tani Bunchō (Nos. 34 & 35). The row of trees in the foreground are reminiscent of Bunchō, but the sharp, delicate nature of the brushwork reflects Nanmei's personal style.

44 Takahisa Aigai   1796-1843
Bamboo and Rocks, 1832
Folding fan, ink on paper, 28.7 x 45.7 cm.
Signature: Aigai Takahisachō
Seals: Chō, Kōho

Inscription: Painted during the first ten days of the twelfth
    month in 1832. Sending pictorial tidings of Heian (Kyoto)
    to Rinsai, my learned friend of the Eastern capital (Edo).
The Metropolitan Museum of Art, New York.
The Harry G. C. Packard Collection of Asian Art, Gift of
    Harry G. C. Packard and Purchase, Fletcher, Rogers,
    Harris Brisbane Dick and Louis V. Bell Funds, Joseph
    Pulitzer Bequest and The Annenberg Fund, Inc.
    Gift, 1975. (1975.268.123)

A pupil of Tani Bunchō and one of the leading Nanga masters in Edo, Aigai was especially well-known for his paintings of bamboo. Bamboo was considered one of the "four gentlemen," plants that were admired by literati because they shared certain characteristics with virtuous old men. For example, bamboo represents endurance, for it stays green all winter long and its culms bend in the wind without breaking. As a painting subject, bamboo was well-suited to the scholar amateur because the strokes making up the leaves and stems are similar to those used in writing.

Uninhibited by the small format, Aigai chose to paint a rather formal and detailed cluster of bamboo. It springs forth from the ground alongside rocks from Lake T'ai in China, distinguishable by the large holes eroded by water. Such rocks were highly sought after by Chinese petrophiles, and Aigai likely saw them illustrated in manuals of imported Chinese paintings. One of the features of this work is the delicate variation in ink tones which adds a shadowy depth to the setting. Aigai has also achieved a balance and unity of design in this painting through a selective placement of the elements on the curved fan surface. Rocks and bamboo splay outward from the lower fan edge, but near the top they yield to the border by bending right and left, echoing the curved edge of the fan.

45 Murase Taiitsu   1803-1881
My Natural Place
Ink on paper, 25 x 52 cm.
Signature: Taiitsu Rōjin heidai
Seals: Yogi (hobby); second seal undecipherable
Inscription: see text below
Private collection

Published: Milne Henderson, *Nanga Fan Painting*
    (London, 1975), no. 31; Stephen Addiss, *A Japanese
    Eccentric: The Three Arts of Murase Taiitsu* (New Orleans,
    1979), no. 22.

Few fan paintings by Taiitsu survive, but those that do reveal a very personal side of the artist. Born in the village of Kōzuchi (present-day Mino city), Taiitsu received a classic Confucian education and eventually opened his own school in Nagoya. He later transferred to a school in the town of Inuyama. However, the collapse of the Tokugawa government and Meiji restoration in 1868 wrought great changes upon his lifestyle. Feudal clans were abolished and along with them Confucian schools. Taiitsu turned to private tutoring to support himself, and in his newly acquired free time began to devote himself more fully to painting, calligraphy and poetry.

In the center of this fan, a tiny scholar sits inside a thatched hut, gazing wistfully at the distant mountains. The vital presence of nature is felt all around him, from the large trees vigorously curling over the hut, to the bold slashes making up the pine foliage. The bending of the trees and undulating mountains repeat the curved line of the fan, and in the remaining triangular space at the left Taiitsu has compressed the following poem.

> All the methods that restrict man don't apply to me,
> What you see in this painting is my natural place.
> Where peaks and ridges pull back, there is space to ramble;
> Pale ink penetrates the forest, and distant mountains
>   emerge.
> (translated by Stephen Addiss)

MARUYAMA-SHIJŌ

46 Nagasawa Rosetsu   1754-1799
Dragon Emerging from Clouds
Ink on paper, 25.5 x 52 cm.
Signature: Rosetsu sha
Seal: Gyō
The Brooklyn Museum, 81.37

Published: The Brooklyn Museum, *Japanese Paintings and
Prints of the Shijō School* (Brooklyn, 1981), p. 24

Dragons have been a popular subject in painting since ancient times. In Buddhism the dragon was identified with the Indian *naga* and believed to be a supernatural being in serpentine form. Living on the earth, in the sky and in the water, dragons were believed to control the clouds and rain. Writhing dragons became prominent images in Momoyama period painting because they conveyed power and energy, especially when painted in large scale on sliding doors and screens.

In converting this powerful image to the small fan format, the artist imbued his dragon with a touch of whimsy. A pupil of Maruyama Ōkyo, Rosetsu gradually drew away from his mentor and painted in a more lively and sometimes eccentric manner. His works are often light-hearted and playful like this dragon, and feature startlingly bold brush effects. Here the dragon's head and claw were delineated with a few freely brushed lines, then wet washes were boldly applied to suggest the body and perhaps sky. This fan presents a smaller version of the dragon painted by Rosetsu on sliding doors at Mūryōji in Wakayama prefecture which also features only the dragon's head and one claw.

47 Nagasawa Rosetsu   1754-1799
Landscape
Hanging scroll, ink on mica-treated paper, 18.3 x 49.2 cm.
Signature: Heian Rosetsu sha
Seal: Gyō
Shōka collection

Published: Robert Moes, *Rosetsu* (Denver, 1973), no. 34.

Rosetsu was exceptionally skillful at handling ink wash, exemplified in this evocative landscape painting. Broad strokes of wet ink were used to create the unusually shaped mountain in the center, and lighter washes suggest the distant peaks across the lake. The empty space around them becomes water, mist and sky. At the water's edge sits a tiny fishing village. Several men are pulling in a small boat at the left, and on the opposite side is a boat which is homeward bound. There is a harmony between line and areas of wash, and the concentration of linework in the lower left is nicely balanced by the signature in the upper right. The velvety washes are enhanced by the mica-treated paper which adds a lustrous finish.

48 Watanabe Nangaku   1767-1813
Courtesan in Boat
Ink and color on paper, 17.5 x 48 cm.
Signature: Nangaku
Seal: Cypher
Cornelius and Shizuko Ouwehand-Kusunoki collection

Born in Kyoto, Nangaku was a pupil of Maruyama Ōkyo (1733-1795) and learned to paint soft, naturalistic pictures of beautiful women in the tradition of his master. However, Nangaku also developed a more abbreviated, lighthearted style of painting which can be observed in this fan. Here Nangaku has depicted a theme known as *Asazumabune,* with a courtesan dressed in Heian period attire seated in a boat with a small drum. The style of her white robes and unusual hat indicate that the courtesan is a performer of *shirabyōshi,* a kind of entertainment which consisted of dancing while chanting Heian style poetry. The subject was popularized in the Genroku era by the artist Hanabusa Itchō (1652-1724), who specialized in figures and genre painting. Nangaku's training in the Maruyama tradition

is evident in the courtesan's hat and the boat which are rendered entirely with washes applied with an unevenly inked brush. This in combination with the animated linework imbues the painting with a refreshing spontaneity.

49 Shibata Gitō   1780-1819
Two Dancers
Ink and light color on paper, 18 x 51.2 cm.
Signature: Gitō
Seals: Gi, tō
Private collection

Shibata Gitō, a pupil of Matsumura Goshun, was trained in the Shijō style. Although his career was cut short by an early death, he left a number of paintings characterized by soft, eloquent brushwork. Gitō's remarkable sense of design is evident in this fan in which two figures perform *kakubē-jishi.* Wearing carved wooden lion masks on top of their heads, itinerant entertainers performed this half-dance, half-tumbling act to the beat of small drums held at their stomachs.

Springing upward from the lower axis of the fan, the dancers are positioned with their backs to one another, their bodies forming gentle curves. One faces right and the other left, enticing the viewer to follow the line of movement in both directions. Angular lines were avoided in favor of rounded ones, the linear rhythms are smooth and flowing. In particular, the long brushstrokes protruding from the headdresses are extraordinarily free and full of vigor. Much of the charm of this work derives from its feeling of spontaneous joy, a quality which was cherished by masters of the Shijō school.

50 Ōnishi Chinnen   1792-1851
Mount Fuji
Folding fan, ink on paper, 15 x 44 cm.
Signature: Chinnen
Seal: Sonan
The Ashmolean Museum

Published: Carol Dorrington-Ward, *Fans from the East* (New York, 1978), no. 19.

The shape of Mount Fuji is particularly well-suited to the fan format, for its triangular peak can be boldly silhouetted against the curved background. Chinnen has deliberately placed the mountain slightly to the left to avoid obvious symmetry. One can imagine the pleasure of fanning oneself on a hot summer day while recalling the cool breezes atop Mount Fuji

A samurai living in Edo, Chinnen was in charge of the rice graineries of the Tokugawa government. He studied painting with both Watanabe Nangaku and Tani Bunchō, but the Shijō style of the former seems to have had a stronger influence. Here Chinnen has reduced Mount Fuji to a few bold sweeps of ink wash. While the surface was

still wet, more ink was dropped on the fan which pooled and created the marvelous blurred textures which are an important feature in the overall design. This fan painting is simple, yet monumental in conception, and the ease and fluency of handling the brush mark it as the product of a mature artist.

51 Kishi Renzan   1804-1859
Boatmen in a Winter Landscape, 1852
Ink and light color on paper, 18.7 x 46.8 cm.
Signature: Renzan(?)
Seal: Gantoku
Inscription: Done in the Kaei era, 1852
Private collection

Renzan was the pupil and adopted son of Kishi Ganku, founder of the Kishi school, a sub-branch of the Maruyama-Shijō tradition of painting. One characteristic feature of this school is the vigorous, often tremulous brushwork which can be seen here in the jagged branches of snow-covered trees. Snow has been suggested by leaving areas of empty paper around the trees, huts and other landscape elements. Around the edges of white paper Renzan applied cool blue and gray washes which succeed in evoking the icy chill of winter.

Amidst this snowy scene, two boats move slowly down the river toward the right, poled by figures dressed in straw hats and coats. The line of movement is repeated in the branches of the darkly inked tree in the middle right, and again in the crevice of the distant hills. The variety of contrasts are what make this painting so successful: the dark ink versus white paper, the angular lines versus curved fan shape, and the sharp, bristly quality of the branches versus the soft blanket of white snow.

52 Shibata Zeshin   1807-1891
Seascape with Gulls and Waves
From an album of 12 fan paintings in watercolor and
    touches of gold on paper, 16 x 48.3 cm.
Signature: Zeshin
Seal: undecipherable
Seattle Art Museum, Eugene Fuller Memorial Collection,
    61.80.8

Published: Henry Trubner, et al., *Asiatic Art in the Seattle Art Museum* (Seattle, 1973), no. 236; Gōke Tadaomi, ed., *Shibata Zeshin meihin shū* (Tokyo, 1981), vol. 1, no. 302.

The theme of birds flying over waves has been popular for centuries in Japanese art. The undulating waves and arched wings of the birds are well suited to the fan format since the forms repeat the fan's crescent shape. Zeshin has dramatized the flight of birds by the background of vivid blue. Slender strokes of gold color delineate the waves, and in the center white paint has been splashed on to simulate the white foam created by the frothing waves.

Shibata Zeshin was one of the most active artists at the
end of the Edo and early Meiji periods. Born in Edo, as a
child he was apprenticed to a lacquer craftsman. He then
became a pupil of the Shijō artist Suzuki Nanrei, and later
went to Kyoto to study with Nanrei's teacher, Okamoto
Toyohiko. The energy with which Zeshin approached his
art was boundless, and his merits were honored by the
Emperor Meiji.

53 Shibata Zeshin   1807-1891
Pine Trees in the Gorge
Hanging scroll, ink and lacquer on paper, 26.6 x 25 cm.
Signature: Zeshin
Seal: Shin
Shin'enKan collection (not in exhibition)

Published: *Japanese Paintings from the Collection of Joe D. Price*
(Lawrence, Kansas, 1967), no. 28; Jack Hillier,
The Uninhibited Brush (London, 1975), no. 274;
Gōke Tadaomi, ed., *Shibata Zeshin meihin shū*
(Tokyo, 1981), vol. 1, no. 55.

Perhaps Zeshin's greatest contribution to the painting
world were his *urushi-e* or lacquer pictures. Ordinarily,
lacquer is applied to a wooden base, but he experimented
with the application of colored lacquers to paper and silk.
Zeshin discovered how to prepare and apply a lacquer
flexible and strong enough to withstand cracking when
unrolled or fading when exposed to strong light. This landscape is one of his outstanding examples in this medium.
Lacquer has been mixed with ink, resulting in the deep rich
brown color with a special sheen. On the surfaces of the
rocks, he has applied it so thickly that it has a smooth,
polished finish. In contrast, the surrounding mist and clouds
are soft and nebulous. Few other artists could master this
technique and Zeshin's lacquer paintings are highly ac-
claimed both in Japan and in the West.

SELECTED BIBLIOGRAPHY

Carol Dorrington-Ward, ed., *Fans from the East* (New York:
Viking Press, 1978).

Tseng Yu-ho Ecke, *Poetry on the Wind* (Honolulu: Honolulu
Academy of Arts, 1982).

Marc S. Gernstein, "Paul Gauguin's Arearea," *Bulletin*,
The Museum of Fine Arts, Houston, Texas, n.s. vol. VII,
no. 4 (fall 1981).

Milne Henderson, *Nanga Fan Painting* (London: Milne
Henderson, 1975).

Jack Hiller, *Japanese Drawings of the 18th and 19th Centuries*
(Washington, D.C.: International Exhibitions Foundation,
1980).

Neville John Irons, *Fans of Imperial China* (Hong Kong:
Kaiserreich Kunst, c. 1981).

Neville John Irons, *Fans of Imperial Japan* (Hong Kong:
Kaiserreich Kunst, 1982).

Hiroshi Mizuo, *Ōgi-e meihin shū* (Kyoto: Tankoshinsha, 1967).

Hiroshi Mizuo, *Sōtatsu Kōrin ha senmen gashū* (Kyoto: Korin
Publishing Company, Ltd., 1965).

Ōta Memorial Art Museum, *Collection of Fan Paintings*,
Volume 2 Edo Rimpa (Tokyo: Ōta Memorial Art
Museum, 1982).